The Royal Court Theatre and Playful Productions present

The Unbelievers

By Nick Payne

The Unbelievers was first performed at the Royal Court Jerwood Theatre Downstairs on Friday 10 October 2025.

The Unbelievers
By Nick Payne

Cast (in alphabetical order)

PC Angela Fisher/ Mia Olsson **Isabel Adomakoh Young**
Nancy Gomez **Alby Baldwin**
David Wright **Paul Higgins**
Margaret Wright **Ella Lily Hyland**
Benjamin **Harry Kershaw**
Karl Gomez **Martin Marquez**
PC Jay Shah/Anil **Jaz Singh Deol**
DC Elizabeth Hawkins/Lorraine **Lucy Thackeray**
Miriam Wright **Nicola Walker**

Director **Marianne Elliott**
Designer **Bunny Christie**
Lighting Designer **Jack Knowles**
Composer & Sound Designer **Nicola T. Chang**
Movement Director **Etta Murfitt**
Casting Director **Charlotte Sutton CDG**
Design Associate **Verity Sadler**
Assistant Director **Anna Hampton**
Props Supervisor **Lily Mollgaard**
Voice **Hazel Holder**
Casting Associate **Saffeya Shebli**
Production Manager **Zara Drohan**
Costume Supervisor **Lucy Walshaw**
Company Manager **Mica Taylor**
Stage Manager **Laura Draper**
Deputy Stage Manager **Surenee Somchit**
Assistant Stage Manager **Ava G. McCarthy**
Stage Supervisor **Steve Evans**
Stage Show Technician **Oscar Sale**
Lighting Supervisor **Lucinda Plummer**
Lighting Programmer **Lizzie Skellett**
Lighting Operator **Holly Higgs**
Dresser **Katie Pollard**
Set Build **Illusion Design & Construct**
Lead Producer **Hannah Lyall**
Executive Producer **Steven Atkinson**

The Royal Court and Stage Management wish to thank the following for their help with this production: Belen Pavani-Sattin from Missing People, Chris Minnighan from the Metropolitan Police Service, Damon Simms from the Society for Psychical Research, Gillian Matini from the College of Psychic Studies.

Nick Payne (Writer)

For the Royal Court: **Constellations, The Art of Dying, Wanderlust, The Lost Mariner (Rough Cut), Starlings (Young Writers Festival Reading).**

Other theatre includes: **A Life (& Public, New York), Constellations (& West End) (Broadway); Elegy, The Same Deep Water As Me (Donmar); Blurred Lines (Shed/National); Lay Down Your Cross (Hampstead); One Day When We Were Young (Paines Plough/Sheffield Theatres); Incognito (& HighTide/Manhattan Theatre Club, New York), If There Is I Haven't Found It Yet (& Roundabout, New York) (Bush).**

Television includes: **Wanderlust, The Secrets.**

Film includes: **We Live in Time, Midwinter Break, The Sense of an Ending, Nora.**

Awards include: **Evening Standard Theatre Award for Best New Play (Constellations), Pearson Playwright-in-Residence at the Bush Theatre, George Devine Award for Most Promising Playwright.**

Isabel Adomakoh Young
(Performer)

For the Royal Court: **Living Newspaper.**

Other theatre includes: **0800 Cupid (THISISPOPBABY), Listen Dance (Little Bulb), As You Like It (The Globe), Modest (UK Tour, Kiln), Hamlet (Bristol Old Vic), Dear Elizabeth (Gate Theatre), Meatballs (Hampstead Theatre), The Provoked Wife, Venice Preserved (RSC); Bite Your Tongue (Hackney Showroom/Talawa), Brood (Arcola); The 80s Show (The Glory).**

Television includes: **Eastenders, Cheaters, Heartstopper and Foundation.**

Alby Baldwin (Performer)

Theatre includes: **Hamlet Hail to the Thief, Julius Caesar (RSC); Tender, Paradise Now! (Bush); Through the Cracks (ETT); Antigone (Holy What); Wild Swimming (Full Rogue); Harry Potter and the Cursed Child, Pride & Prejudice (*Sort Of) (West End); The Wolves (Stratford East); Dear Elizabeth (Gate); Chatter (CPT); The Reasons (New Diorama); Love Scenes for the End of the World, how to build a wax figure (November Theatre); Scripted (Sheffield Crucible).**

Film includes: **Love Wins.**

Television includes: **The Great, I Hate Suzie, The Jewish Enquirer.**

Radio includes: **V, Homebody, Persuasion, Our Wives Under the Sea, Experienced, Faking It, Homebody.**

Nicola T. Chang
(Composer & Sound Designer)

For the Royal Court: **For Black Boys Who Have Considered Suicide When the Hue Gets Too Heavy (& New Diorama & West End), White Pearl, Sound of the Underground.**

Other theatre includes: **My Neighbour Totoro (& Gillian Lynne/Barbican), All Mirth and No Matter (RSC); The Importance of Being Earnest, Kerry Jackson (National), Skeleton Crew (Donmar); Minority Report (Nottingham Playhouse/Birmingham Rep/Lyric Hammersmith); A Midsummer Night's Dream, The Death of Ophelia (The Globe); Escaped Alone & What If If Only (Manchester Royal Exchange); Tribe, Of the Cut (Young Vic); Shanghai Dolls, The Ministry of Lesbian Affairs (& Soho), The Ballad of Hattie and James (Kiln); The Swell, Little Baby Jesus (Orange Tree); A Playlist for the Revolution, Communion (Bush); Feral Monster (National Theatre of Wales); A Doll's House (Crucible, Sheffield); Reverberation (Bristol Old Vic); Dziady (Almeida); How I Learned to Swim (Paines Plough/tour).**

Film includes: **If You Only Knew, Mei, BakedBeans, Twitching, The Fight in the Dog, The Bicycle, Devi, IRL, LAID, Getting Away with Murder(s), Seafruit, A Dose of Happiness, Boundaries, You Wouldn't Adam and Eve It, Postcards from the 48%, The Perfect Dinner.**

Awards include: **Evening Standard Future Theatre Fund for Best Audio Design (Audio Design).**

Bunny Christie (Designer)

For the Royal Court: **Haunted Child, Kin, Babies, Terrible Voice of Satan, Gibraltar Strait, Man to Man.**

Other theatre includes: **After Life, London Tide, People, Places and Things, The Curious Incident of the Dog in the Night-Time, The Red Barn, Emil and the Detectives, The White Guard, The Cherry Orchard, Comedy of Errors, The Welkin (National); Guys and Dolls, A Midsummer Night's Dream (Bridge); Company (& Broadway), Best of Enemies (& Young Vic) (West End); Tammy Faye (& Broadway), The Wild Duck, Ink (& Broadway) (Almeida).**

Opera includes: **Brief Encounter, Tosca (Houston Grand Opera); Medea (English National Opera/Geneva Grand Opera).**

Awards include: **Olivier Award for Best Set Design (Company), Tony Award for Best ScenicDesign in a Play (The Curious Incident of the Dog in the Night-Time), Olivier Award for Best Set Design (The Curious Incident of the Dog in the Night-Time), Olivier Award for Best Set Design (The White Guard), Olivier Award for Best Set Design (A Streetcar Named Desire).**

At the National Theatre she initiated their Design Bursary. Bunny is a Director of Scene-Change a Collective of Theatre Designers. She was awarded an OBE for services to the UK Theatre Industry.

Jaz Singh Deol (Performer)

For the Royal Court: **The Djinns of Eidgah, Linda.**

Other theatre includes: **Marriage Material (Lyric Hammersmith); Tartuffe (Haymarket Theatre); Lions and Tigers (Sam Wanamaker); Snookered (Bush); Mush and Me (Adelaide Festival).**

Television includes: **Toxic Town, EastEnders, The Sister Boniface Mysteries, The Boy with the Top Knot, Lovesick, Code of a Killer, The Halcyon, Love, Lies and Records.**

Film includes: **The Killer, Terminal, Viceroy's House, Darkness Visible.**

Laura Draper (Stage Manager)

For the Royal Court: **Glass. Kill. Bluebeard. Imp, The Cane, The Woods, The Children, Torn, Hope, Love and Information, Vera, Vera, Vera, The Heretic, Chicken Soup with Barley.**

Other theatre includes: **The Brightening Air, Groundhog Day, A Number, Girl from the North Country (& West End) (Old Vic), Coriolanus, The House of Bernarda Alba, Jack Absolute Flies Again, Top Girls, Julie, The Deep Blue Sea (National); Long Day's Journey Into Night, The Comeback, The Father (West End); Natasha, Pierre and the Great Comet of 1812, Fathers and Sons, Versailles, The Night Alive, Trelawny of the Wells, The Physicists (Donmar); A Midsummer Night's Dream, Happy Days (Young Vic); A Streetcar Named Desire, Little Eyolf, Bakkhai, Ghosts (& BAM), The Dark Earth Light and The Light Sky, Reasons To Be Pretty (Almeida).**

Marianne Elliott (Director)

For the Royal Court: **Stoning Mary, Notes on Falling Leaves, The Sugar Syndrome.**

Other theatre includes: **Cock, Death of a Salesman (& Young Vic), Company (& Broadway), Hesienberg (West End); Angels in America (& Broadway), Husbands and Sons, Rules for Living, The Light Princess, Port, Curious Incident of the Dog in the Night-Time (& West End/Broadway), Season's Greetings, Women Beware Women, All's Well That Ends Well, Mrs Affleck, Harper Regan, War Horse (& West End/Broadway), Saint Joan, Therese Raquin, Pillars of the Community (National); Sweet Bird of Youth (Old Vic); Much Ado About Nothing (RSC); Port, Design for Living, Les Blancs, As You Like It, A Woman of No Importance, Nude with Violin, Fast Food, Martin Yesterday, Poor Super Man, Mad for It, The Deep Blue Sea, I Have Been Here Before (Royal Exchange); The Little Foxes (Donmar); Terracotta (Hampstead/Birmingham Rep).**

Television includes: **Talking Heads.**

Film includes: **The Salt Path, Alice.**

Awards include: **Olivier Award for Best Director (Death of a Salesman); Olivier Award for Best Musical Revival, Evening Standard Theatre Award for Best Director (Company); Tony Award for Best Revival, Olivier Award for Best Revival, Outer Critics Circle Award for Outstanding Revival of a Play, Drama League Award for Outstanding Revival of a Play, Drama Desk Award for Outstanding Revival of a Play (Angels in America); Olivier Award for Best Director, Tony Award for Best Direction of a Play, Drama Desk Award for Outstanding Director of a Play (The Curious Incident of the Dog in the Night-Time); Tony Award for Best Direction of a Play, Outer Critics Circle for Outstanding Director of a Play (War Horse); Evening Standard Theatre Award for Best Director (Pillars of the Community).**

Marianne was awarded an OBE for her Services to Theatre.

Anna Hampton (Assistant Director)

As assistant director, theatre includes: **Orpheus Descending (Cockpit); Berlusconi (Southwark Playhouse); The Lower Depths, Mosquitoes, London (LAMDA); Antigonick (Torn Out).**

As director, theatre includes: **Machinal (Orange Tree); The Underneath (Edinburgh Fringe); Soultide (Etcetera); It's Casual (Canal Cafe); Three's a Crowd, Dogs and Trees (LAMDA); A Funny Thing Happened On the Way to the Gynecologic Oncology Unit, Do Big Kids Cry? (Polaris North); Stupid F*cking Bird, Hedda Gabler, Far Away (Kenyon College).**

Paul Higgins (Performer)

For the Royal Court: **Hope, Nightsongs, American Bagpipes, Conquest of the South Pole, A Wholly Healthy Glasgow.**

Other theatre includes: **The Seagull (Barbican); Romeo and Juliet, The Doctor, Macbeth, Conversations After a Burial (Almeida); Local Hero (Chichester Festival); This is Memorial Device (Traverse/ Tron/ Riverside); The Meaning of Zong (Bristol Old Vic); Aristocrats, Temple, Luise Miller, The Cosmonaut's Last Message... (Donmar); The Seagull (Lyric Hammersmith); Twilight Song (Park); Blackbird, King Lear (Citizens Theatre); Children of the Sun, Caledonia, The White Guard, Paul, An Enemy of the People (& Ahmanson, LA), The Hare Trilogy (National); Damascus (Traverse/ Kiln); Black Watch (National Theatre of Scotland); The Tempest (Tron); Measure for Measure (RSC); A Midsummer Night's Dream (Globe); Buried Alive (Hampstead); The Way of the World, Romeo & Juliet, A View from the Bridge (Royal Exchange); The Slab Boys Trilogy (Young Vic).**

Television includes: **The Simpsons, Slow Horses, The Ipcress Files, Beep, Cold Call, Line of Duty, Raised by Wolves, Utopia, The Last Enemy, The Thick of It, Low Winter Sun, Staying Alive.**

Film includes: **Kill, Greed, Apostle, The Party's Just Beginning, Couple in a Hole, Victoria and Abdul, In The Loop, The Red Road, Complicity, Bedrooms and Hallways.**

Hazel Holder (Voice Coach)

For the Royal Court: **Giant, seven methods of killing kylie jenner, A Kind of People, Poet in Da Corner, Cuttin' It (& Young Vic/Birmingham Rep/Sheffield Theatres/Yard), Grimly Handsome, ear for eye, Father Comes Home from the Wars (Parts 1, 2 & 3), Pigs & Dogs.**

Other theatre includes: **Alterations, The Importance of Being Earnest, A Tupperware of Ashes, The Grapes of Wrath, The Hot Wing King, People, Places & Things (& Trafalgar Studios), Death of England: Closing Time, The Effect, Grenfell: in the words of survivors, Blues for an Alabama Sky, Small Island, Trouble in Mind, Rockets and Blue Lights, Death of England, Pericles, Julie, Nine Night (& West End), Barber Shop Chronicles, Angels in America, Les Blancs, Ma Rainey's Black Bottom, wonder.land** (National); **Passing Strange, The Homecoming, Mandela, Changing Destiny, Fairview, Death of a Salesman (& West End), The Convert. The Mountaintop, The Emperor** (Young Vic); **Two Strangers (Carry a Cake Across New York) (& West End), Mlima's Tale, Retrograde, Retrograde, The Wife of Willesden, Pass Over, The Son** (Kiln);**Stereophonic, Barcelona, Long Days Journey Into Night, Opening Night, Enemy of the People, Ulster American, Sunset Boulevard, Best of Enemies, The Glass Menagerie, To Kill a Mockingbird, Cock, 2:22 A Ghost Story, Get Up Stand Up! The Bob Marley Musical, Constellations (& Donmar), Uncle Vanya, Tina – The Tina Turner Musical, Matilda, Aladdin [Stand In], The Goat, or Who Is Sylvia, Dreamgirls** (West End); **The Human Body, Clyde's, A Doll's House Part II, Marys Seacole, Love and Other Acts of Violence, [BLANK]** (Donmar); **Rock 'n' Roll, Death of a Black Man, Caroline, or Change (& West End/Chichester Festival)** (Hampstead); **August in England, Leave Taking, F**k The Polar Bears** (Bush); **Newsies** (Troubadour); **Jitney, Misanthropes** (Old Vic); **Blue/Orange (& Oxford Playhouse/Theatre Royal Bath), Our Lady of Kibeho, Soul** (Royal & Derngate); **White Noise, A Very Very Very Dark Matter** (Bridge); **The Gift** (Belgrade); **Richard II** (Globe); **The Madness of George III, Shebeen (& Stratford East)** (Nottingham Playhouse); **Death of a Salesman** (Royal Exchange); **Little Shop of Horrors, Peter Pan** (Regents Park Open Air); **Twilight LA, Eclipsed, The Rise & Shine of Comrade Fiasco** (Gate); **Black Men Walking (& Eclipse), Guys and Dolls (& Talawa)** (Royal Exchange); **The Rolling Stone** (Orange Tree/Royal Exchange); **Rites** (NTS); **The Initiate** (Paines Plough).

Television includes: **A Thousand Blows, Silo, The Power, The Baby, Small Axe.**

Film includes: **The Ministry of Ungentlemanly Warfare, Aisha, ear for eye, The Silent Twins, Death on the Nile.**

Ella Lily Hyland (Performer)

Theatre includes: **Grania (Abbey).**

Television includes: **Towards Zero, Black Doves, Wrapped, A Thousand Blows, Fifteen-Love.**

Film includes: **Silent Roar.**

Harry Kershaw (Performer)

Theatre includes: **Our Country's Good (Lyric Hammersmith), Fanny (Watermill Theatre), Peter Pan Goes Wrong (Broadway/LA/West End), Good Luck Studio (UK Tour), Boris III (Edinburgh), What's New Pussycat, Edmond De Bergerac (Birmingham Rep), The Madness Of George III (Nottingham Playhouse/ NT Live), This House (National Theatre/Headlong), Mischief Movie Night The Play That Goes Wrong, One Man Two Guvnors (West End).**

Film includes: **Skyfall, Great Expectations, Exhibition, Unrelated, Office Royale.**

Television includes: **Jerk, Cuckoo, Endeavour, The Interceptor, Switch, Omid Djalili's Little Crackers, Wallander.**

Jack Knowles (Lighting Designer)

For the Royal Court: **Glass. Kill. Bluebeard. Imp, The End of History, Instructions for Correct Assembly, 2071 (& Schauspielhaus Hamburg).**

Other theatre includes: **Every Brilliant Thing (@sohoplace); A Moon for the Misbegotten, 1536, Patriots (& Broadway/ Noël Coward), Spring Awakening, Carmen Disruption (Almeida); Sunset Boulevard (Broadway/Savoy); Two Strangers (Carry a Cake Across New York) (A.R.T/Criterion/Kiln); London Tide, Romeo and Julie, Barber Shop Chronicles (& International Tour), Top Girls, Beginning (& Ambassadors), Cleansed (National); Much Ado About Nothing, Hamlet, Venice Preserved (Royal Shakespeare Company); Long Day's Journey Into Night (Wyndham's); Best of Enemies (Noël Coward); Caroline, or Change (Broadway/ Playhouse); The Lion, the Witch and the Wardrobe (Gillian Lynne/UK Tour); Private Lives, Committee (Donmar); Light Falls, The Producers, Happy Days (Royal Exchange); Julie (Internationaal Theater Amsterdam); 4.48 Psychosis, Happy Days, Travelling on One Leg (Schauspielhaus Hamburg); Salt of the Earth (Venice Biennale); The Night Train (Schauspiel Köln); Lungs (Schaubühne Berlin).**

Opera includes: **La bohéme (Göteborgsoperan), The Seven Deadly Sins/Bluebeard's Castle (Teatro Colón).**

Awards include: **Tony Award for Best Lighting Design of a Musical, Olivier Award for Best Lighting Design, Drama Desk Award for Best Lighting Design of a Musical, WhatsOnStage Award for Best Lighting Design (Sunset Boulevard), Knight of Illumination Award (Barber Shop Chronicles).**

Martin Marquez (Performer)

For the Royal Court: **Stoning Mary, Identical Twins, Cleansed.**

Other theatre includes: **Dear England, Othello, This House, Husbands and Sons, Mother Courage and Her Children, Anything Goes (& West End) and Love's Labour's Lost** (National); **A View from the Bridge, Brokeback Mountain, From Here to Eternity, Macbeth** (West End); **Ah, Wilderness!** (Young Vic); **Blasted** (Sheffield Theatres); **The Crucible, Of Mice and Men and Don Juan** (West Yorkshire Playhouse); **I Caught My Death in Venice, Gondoliers, Pal Joey and Insignificance** (Chichester Festival); **Snowbull** (Hampstead); **Brothers Marquez** (Soho); **Four Nights in Knaresborough** (Kiln); **The Iceman Cometh** (Old Vic); **The Front Page, Fool for Love** (Donmar); **Jude the Obscure, Private Lives and Flesh & Blood for Method & Madness;** and **Hamlet, A View from the Bridge, The Slicing Edge and Road** (New Wolsey, Ipswich).

Television includes: **Doc Martin, Kate and Koji, The Chelsea Detective, The Crown, Woody, Vera, Falcon, Holy Flying Circus, New Tricks, Hotel Babylon, Waking the Dead Lead Balloon, Elizabeth, Empire and Heartbeat.** Film includes: **Les Misérables, The Business.**

Film includes: **Les Misérables, The Business.**

Ava G. McCarthy (Assistant Stage Manager)

For the Royal Court: **Word-Play, One Night Stands.**

Other theatre includes: **The Play That Goes Wrong** (West End); **Audiomoves** (Peut-Etre); **The Government Inspector** (Chichester); **Otherland, Look Back In Anger/Roots, King Lear, Portia Coughlan** (Almeida); **FATF (Factory International/Tour); Kiss Marry Kill** (Dante or Die/Tour).

As props supervisor, theatre includes: **Men & Girls Dance** (Fevered Sleep Co.).

Lily Mollgaard (Props Supervisor)

For the Royal Court: **Giant (& West End).**

Other theatre includes: **My Neighbour Totoro** (RSC); **The Car Man** (Royal Albert Hall); **Guys and Dolls, Straight Line Crazy, John Gabriel Borkman, The Southbury Child, A Number, Beat The Devil, Talking Heads, Bach and Sons, The Book of Dust – La Belle Sauvage, Julius Caesar, Night Fall and A Midsummer Night's Dream** (Bridge); **Matthew Bourne's New Adventures** (Sadler's Wells/Tour); **Peaky Blinders** (Tour); **Tammy Faye, The Wild Duck** (Almeida); **Lion King, Sunset Boulevard (& Broadway), Bombay Dreams (& Broadway), Joseph, Made in Dagenham, The Producers, Oliver!, Shrek, Miss Saigon, Spamalot, Sister Act, Hairspray, School of Rock, Company, The Pinter Season One, Two, Five and Six, Cyrano de Bergerac (& Jamie Lloyd), Leopoldstadt (& Sonia Friedman), Prince of Egypt, 9 to 5** (West End); **Jesus Christ Superstar** (Broadway/Tour); **Evita** (Regent's Park Open Air); **Blithe Spirit** (Theatre Royal Bath).

Etta Murfitt (Movement Director)

As associate artistic director of New Adventures, dance includes: **The Midnight Bell, Romeo and Juliet, The Red Shoes, Swan Lake, Early Adventures, Cinderella, Dorian Gray, Edward Scissorhands, Highland Fling, Nutcracker!, The Car, The Infernal Galop, The Percys of Fitzrovia, Deadly Serious, Town and Country.**

Choreography credits include: **North By Northwest, The Buddha of Suburbia (& RSC/Barbican), Blue Beard (Wise Children/Tour); Oliver!, Rosencrantz and Guildenstern are dead (& Haymarket Theatre) (Chichester); Wuthering Heights (National/Tour); Bagdad Café, Wise Children(& Tour) (Old Vic); Romantics Anonymous (Bristol Old Vic/Sam Wanamaker); Orpheus in the Underworld (ENO); A Clockwork Orange (Everyman & Playhouse); The Tin Drum, Umbrellas of Cherbourg, Wild Bride, Midnights Pumpkin (Kneehigh/Tour); Much Ado About Nothing, A Midsummer Night's Dream (Globe); Le Nozze di Figaro (Holland Park); The Way of the World (Wilton's Music Hall); A Midsummer Night's Dream (Albery Theatre); Travesties, Sleeping Beauty (Birmingham Rep).**

Television includes: **Matthew Bourne's Christmas, Storm – Aletta Collins, Swan Lake, Roald Dahl's Red Riding Hood, Nutcracker!, The Car Man.**

Film includes: **Late Flowering Lust, Mrs Hartley and the Growth Centre.**

Verity Sadler (Design Associate)

Theatre includes: **London Tide, People, Places and Things (& Tour) (National); Guys & Dolls (Bridge); Best of Enemies (Young Vic); Tammy Faye, Ink (& West End) (Almeida); Company (West End/Broadway).**

As set and costume designer, theatre includes: **Noiseboys (Fringe).**

As costume and co-set designer, theatre includes: **The Choir of Man (Arts/Tour); Extravaganza Macabre, When Autumn Turns to Winter and Antarctica (Little Bulb).**

As costume supervisor, theatre includes: **Lost & Found (Factory International); Red Riding (Stratford East); The Last Ship (Tour); Space Shed (Unlimited); Poppea (Trinity Laban); Missing for Gecko, Stowaway for Analogue, Holes, One Million, Burntwater (Tangled Feet).**

Television includes: **Hansel & Gretel, Thumbelina, The Snow Queen, The Nutcracker, Alice in Wonderland, Peter Pan, A Christmas Carol (CBeebies).**

Film includes: **Macbeth, Blitz, Hamlet and Mr Nice.**

Surenee Somchit
(Deputy Stage Manager)

For the Royal Court: **White Pearl, Hole, The Prudes, Girls & Boys.**

Other theatre includes: **Brigadoon, 101 Dalmatians** (Regent's Park); **Hamlet Hail to the Thief** (& Factory International), **The Buddha of Suburbia** (RSC); **Natasha, Pierre & the Great Comet of 1812, Berberian Sound Studio, The Lady from the Sea** (Donmar); **The Real Thing** (Old Vic); **The Witches, Grenfell: in the words of survivors, Three Sisters, Barber Shop Chronicles, Twelfth Night, Les Blancs, I Want My Hat Back, Pomona, We Want You to Watch** (National); **The Secret Life of Bees, Tammy Faye, Spring Awakening, Dance Nation** (Almeida); **Cock** (Elliott & Harper); **Anna X, Merrily We Roll Along** (& Menier Chocolate Factory) (SFP); **The Night of the Iguana** (Fiery Angel); **Once in a Lifetime** (Young Vic); **Eclipsed** (Gate); **Oh What a Lovely War** (Theatre Royal Stratford East).

Charlotte Sutton CDG
(Casting Director)

Theatre includes: **Hamlet Hail to the Thief** (& Factory International), **Hamlet, The Red Shoes, Pericles, Love's Labour's Lost** (RSC); **Guys and Dolls** (Bridge); **The Unfriend** (Wyndham's/ Criterion/ Chichester Festival); **The Secret Life of Bees** (Almeida); **Best of Enemies, Death of a Salesman** (Young Vic/West End); **Further than the Furthest Thing, Fairview, The Convert, trade, Dutchman** (Young Vic); **Our Generation** (Chichester Festival/National); **The Inquiry, Assassins, Local Hero, The Famous Five, Sing Yer Heart Out for the Lads, Doubt, Oklahoma!, The Deep Blue Sea, The Watsons, Cock, Flowers for Mrs Harris, The Meeting, random/generations, Quiz, Fiddler on the Roof, Strife, Mack and Mabel, Caroline, or Change** (& Hampstead/ Playhouse), **South Pacific** (& Sadler's Wells/ UK tour) (Chichester Festival); **Cock** (Ambassadors); **Company** (Gielgud); **Long Day's Journey into Night** (Wyndham's/ BAM/LA); **wonder.land, The Light Princess, Emil and the Detectives, The Elephantom** (National).

Film includes: **Disenchanted** (UK casting), **Mufasa: The Lion King** (Taka Cub and Chigaru Casting).

Awards include: **CDG Award for Best Casting in Musical Theatre (Guys and Dolls), CDG Award for Best Casting in Theatre (Our Generation).**

Lucy Thackeray (Performer)

Theatre includes: **The Buddha of Suburbia (RSC/Wise Children/Barbican); Brief Encounter (West End); A Midsummer Night's Dream (Globe); Heroine (HighTide/Theatre Clwyd); Bike, Fallen Angels (Salisbury Playhouse); Corrie! (UK/New Zealand Tour); Amaka (Jack Studio); My Beautiful Black Dog (Bush); Sweeney Todd, Noises Off, How the Other Half Loves (Queen's Theatre Hornchurch).**

Television includes: **Doctor Who, Until I Kill You, Call the Midwife, Black Ops, Top Boy, Moon Knight, The Walk-in, Eastenders, Casualty, Don't Forget The Driver, Damned, Hatton Garden, New Tricks, The Five, Doctors, The Dumping Ground, Charlie Brooker's How TV Ruined Your Life.**

Film includes: **Jurassic World Rebirth, Surge, IBoy, Absent.**

Nicola Walker (Performer)

For the Royal Court: **The Cane, Relocated, Fresh Kills, Sweetheart, The Libertine/The Man of Mode, Hated Nightfall.**

Other theatre includes: **Unicorn (West End); The Corn is Green, The Curious Incident of the Dog in the Night-Time, Season's Greetings, Gethsemane, Tales from the Vienna Woods, Edmond (National); A View From the Bridge (Young Vic/West End/Broadway); Di and Viv and Rose, The Dead Eye Boy (Hampstead); Mrs Klein, Cloud Nine (Almeida); Modern Dance for Beginners (Soho); Sexual Perversity in Chicago (Sheffield Crucible); A Lie of the Mind, Passion Play (& Comedy Theatre) (Donmar).**

Television includes: **The Split, Barcelona, Mary & George, Annika, Marriage, Unforgotten, Collateral, Inside No. 9, River, Last Tango in Halifax, Babylon, Scott and Bailey, Prisoner's Wives, Heading Out, Inside Men, Spooks, Being Human, Law & Order, Luther, Turn of the Screw, Oliver Twist, Torn, Broken News, People Like Us, The Last Train, Touching Evil.**

Film includes: **Shooting Dogs, Shiner, Four Weddings and a Funeral.**

Awards include: **Olivier Award for Best Supporting Actress (The Curious Incident of the Dog in the Night-Time).**

THE ROYAL COURT THEATRE

The Royal Court Theatre is the writers' theatre. It is a leading force in world theatre for cultivating and supporting writers - undiscovered, emerging and established.

Since 1956, we have commissioned and produced hundreds of writers, from John Osborne to Mohamed-Zain Dada. Royal Court plays from every decade are now performed on stages and taught in classrooms and universities across the globe.

Through the writers, the Royal Court is at the forefront of creating restless, alert, provocative theatre about now. We open our doors to the unheard voices and free thinkers that, through their writing, change our way of seeing.

We strive to create an environment in which differing voices and opinions can co-exist. In current times, it is becoming increasingly difficult for writers to write what they want or need to write without fear, and we will do everything we can to rise above a narrowing of viewpoints. Through all our work, we strive to inspire audiences and influence future writers with radical thinking and provocative discussion.

PLAYFUL PRODUCTIONS

Founded by Matthew Byam Shaw, Nia Janis and Nick Salmon in 2010, Playful Productions is one of the most eminent independent theatre producers in the West End.

Productions as Producer include Born With Teeth (Wyndham's); The Fifth Step (@SohoPlace); Make It Happen (Dundee Rep & Edinburgh International Festival); Dr. Strangelove (Noël Coward & Bord Gáis, Dublin); Macbeth (Harold Pinter); The Artist (Theatre Royal Plymouth); The Unfriend (Chichester Festival, Criterion & Wyndham's); Accidental Death of an Anarchist (Sheffield, Lyric Hammersmith & Theatre Royal Haymarket); A Little Life (Richmond, Harold Pinter & Savoy); Get Up Stand Up! The Bob Marley Musical (Lyric); The Mirror and the Light (Gielgud); Wolf Hall and Bring Up The Bodies (Aldwych & Broadway); The Weir (Wyndham's) and Frost/Nixon (Donmar Warehouse & Gielgud).

Executive Producer work includes the multi-Emmy-award-winning Netflix TV series The Crown based on The Audience which was co-produced by Playful in the West End and on Broadway.

ROYAL COURT SUPPORTERS

Our incredible community of supporters makes it possible for us to achieve our mission of nurturing and platforming writers at every stage of their careers. Our supporters are part of our essential fabric – they help to give us the freedom to take bigger and bolder risks in our work, develop and empower new voices, and create world-class theatre that challenges and disrupts the theatre ecology.

To all our supporters, thank you. You help us to write the future.

PUBLIC FUNDING

Supported using public funding by
ARTS COUNCIL ENGLAND

CORPORATE SPONSORS & SUPPORTERS
Aqua Financial Ltd
Bloomberg Philanthopies
Cadogan
Character 7
Concord Theatricals
Edwardian Hotels, London
Nick Hern Books
Phone Locker
Riverstone Living
Sloane Stanley
Sustainable Wine Solutions
Walpole

TRUSTS & FOUNDATIONS
Backstage Trust
Bruce Wake Charitable Trust
Chalk Cliff Trust
Clare McIntyre's Bursary
Cockayne - Grants for the Arts
The Common Humanity Arts Trust
Cowley Charitable Foundation
David Laing Foundation
The Davidson PlayGC Bursary
The Dominic Webber Trust - Core Values
The Fenton Arts Trust
Foyle Foundation
Genesis Foundation
The Golsoncott Foundation
Jerwood Foundation
John Thaw Foundation
The Katie Bradford Arts Trust
The Lynne Gagliano Writers' Award
The Marlow Trust
Martin Bowley Charitable Trust
Molecule Theatre Ltd
The Noël Coward Foundation
Old Possum's Practical Trust
Richard Radcliffe Charitable Trust
The Royal Borough of Kensington & Chelsea Arts Grant
Rose Foundation
The Thistle Trust
The Thompson Family Charitable Trust
The T.S. Eliot Foundation
Unity Theatre Trust
Y.A.C.K F.O

INDIVIDUAL SUPPORTERS

Artistic Director's Circle

Eric Abraham
Jeremy & Becky Broome
Clyde Cooper
Debbie De Girolamo & Ben Babcock
Dominique & Neal Gandhi
Lydia & Manfred Gorvy
David & Jean Grier
Charles Holloway OBE
Linda Keenan
Brian and Dayna Lee
Andrew Rodger and Ariana Neumann
Jack Thorne & Rachel Mason
Sandra Treagus for ATA Assoc. LTD
Sally Whitehill & Mark Gordon
Anonymous

Writers' Circle

Chris & Alison Cabot
Cas Donald
Robyn Durie
The Hon P N Gibson's Charity Trust
Kater Gordon
Ellie & Roger Guy
Melanie J. Johnson
Nicola Kerr
Héloïse and Duncan Matthews KC
Emma O'Donoghue
Clare Parsons & Tony Langham
Maureen & Tony Wheeler
Anonymous

Directors' Circle

Piers Butler
Fiona Clements
Professor John Collinge
Julian & Ana Garel-Jones
Carol Hall
Dr Timothy Hyde
Elizabeth O'Connor & Adam Bandeen
Rajeev Philip

Platinum Circle

Moira Andreae
Beverley Buckingham
Katie Bullivant
Anthony Burton CBE
Matthew Dean
Lucy & Spencer De Grey
Emily Fletcher
The Edwin Fox Foundation
Beverley Gee
Madeleine Hodgkin
Kate Howe
Roderick & Elizabeth Jack
Susanne Kapoor
David P Kaskel & Christopher A Teano
Peter & Maria Kellner
Frances Lynn
Robert Ledger & Sally Moulsdale
Mrs Janet Martin
Andrew McIver
Barbara Minto
Brian and Meredith Niles
Timothy Prager
Corinne Rooney
Sir Paul & Lady Ruddock
Sir William & Lady Russell
Anita Scott
Bhags Sharma
Dr Wendy Sigle
Rita Skinner
James and Victoria Tanner
Mrs Caroline Thomas
Yannis Vasatis
Ian, Victoria and Lucinda Watson
Sir Robert & Lady Wilson

With thanks to our Silver and Gold Supporters, and our Friends and Good Friends, whose support we greatly appreciate.

With special thanks to our **Production Circle Supporters**
Natasha Cheung
Clyde Cooper
Ana & Julian Garel-Jones
Steve & Lorraine Groves
Melanie J. Johnson
Nicola Kerr

Royal Court Theatre
Sloane Square,
London SW1W 8AS
Tel: 020 7565 5050
info@royalcourttheatre.com
www.royalcourttheatre.com

Artistic Director
David Byrne
Executive Director
Will Young
Artistic Director's Office Manager
Natalie Dodd

Senior Associate Playwright & Dramaturg
Gillian Greer
Associate Playwright & Young Writers' Associate
Beth Flintoff
Associate Playwrights
Mike Bartlett, Ryan Calais Cameron, Vinay Patel, Ishy Din, Nina Segal.
Associate Artist (Art Direction)
Guy J Sanders
New Plays Associate
Laetitia Somé
Resident Director
Aneesha Srinivasan
Artistic Co-ordinator
Ailsa Dann
Playwrights '73 bursary attachment
Tife Kusoro

Head of Producing & Partnerships
Steven Atkinson
Producer
Hannah Lyall
Casting Associate
Saffeya Shebli
New Writers & Participation Producer
Tabitha Hayward
Producing Assistant
Hetty Opayinka

Director of Development
Anuja Batra
Development Manager
Jennifer Lafferty
Development Officers
Ellena Sychrava, Nash Metaxas.

Head of Production
Marius Rønning
Production Manager
Zara Drohan
Company Manager
Mica Taylor ^
Head of Lighting
Deanna Towli
Deputy Head of Lighting
Lucinda Plummer
Lighting Technician
Izzy Hobby
Lighting Programmer
Lizzie Skellett
Head of Stage
Steve Evans
Deputy Head of stage
Maddy Collins
Stage Show Technician
Oscar Sale
Head of Sound
David McSeveney
Deputy Head of Sound
Jet Sharp
Head of Costume
Lucy Walshaw

Director of Marketing & Communications
Rachael Welsh
Marketing Manager
Benjamin McDonald
Digital Lead
Jessica Manu
Digital Content Producer (Videography)
Giovanni Edwards
Marketing Officer
Elizabeth Carpenter
Communications Officer
Natasha Ryszka-Onions
Press & Publicity
Bread and Butter PR

Finance Director
Helen Perryer
Finance Manager
Olivia Amory
Senior Finance & Payroll Officer
Will Dry
Finance & Administration Assistant
Bukola Sonubi

Head of People
Olivia Shaw
People and Governance Coordinator
Ayushi Mahajan

General Manager
Rachel Dudley
Front of House Manager
Jennelle Reece-Gardner
Box Office Manager
Poppy Templeton
Senior Duty House Manager
Ronay Poole
Ushers/Duty House Managers
Emer Halton-O'Mahony, James Wilson.
Box Office and Administration Assistants
William Byam Shaw, Phoebe Coop, Ollie Harrington, Aidan Thompson-Coates.
Stage Door Keepers
James Graham, Léa Jackson, Paul Lovegrove.

Head of Operations & Sustainability
Robert Smael
Senior Bar & Floor Supervisor
Lucy Stepan, Matthew Paul.
Bar & Floor Supervisors
Isa Wood, Eleanor Willis.
General Maintenance Technician
David Brown

Thanks to all of our Ushers and Bar staff.

^ The post of Company Manager is supported by Charles Holloway OBE.

ENGLISH STAGE COMPANY

Honorary Council
**Graham Devlin CBE
Martin Paisner CBE
Joyce Hytner OBE
Phyllida Lloyd CBE**

Council Chairman
Anthony Burton CBE

Members
**Jennette Arnold OBE
Noma Dumezweni
Neal Gandhi
Pamela Jikiemi
Mwenya Kawesha
Mark Ravenhill
Andrew Rodger
Anita Scott
Lord Stewart Wood**

Become a Member of our Supporters' Circle

Our community of supporters is essential to the future and success of the Royal Court.

Thanks to their generosity, we can take bigger and bolder risks in our work and remain the leading force in world theatre for supporting writers.

From £250 a year our Supporters' Circle receive:

- Priority Booking and access to sold-out shows
- Early access to £15 Mondays
- Complimentary tickets and playtexts
- Invitations to Supporters' Receptions,
- Press Night parties and Season Launch events
- Unique insight opportunities such as
- Script Meetings, Set Tours and more

Join Today

Speak to our Box Office team to find out more about our Supporters' Circle levels, or visit royalcourttheatre.com/support-us.

The English Stage Company at the Royal Court Theatre is a registered charity (No. 231242)

The Unbelievers

Nick Payne's plays include *If There Is I Haven't Found It Yet* (Bush Theatre, London, and Roundabout Theatre Company, New York; winner of the 2009 George Devine Award for Most Promising Playwright); *Wanderlust* (Royal Court Theatre, London); *Sophocles' Electra* (Gate Theatre, London); *Lay Down Your Cross* (Hampstead Theatre Downstairs, London); *One Day When We Were Young* (Paines Plough/Sheffield Theatres); *Constellations* (Broadway, Royal Court Theatre, Duke of York's and UK tour; winner of the 2012 Evening Standard Theatre Award for Best Play, nominated for 2013 Olivier Award for Best New Play); *The Same Deep Water As Me* (Donmar Warehouse, London; nominated for 2014 Olivier Award for Best New Comedy); *Blurred Lines* (The Shed, National Theatre, London); *Incognito* (Nabokov/Live Theatre, Newcastle, Bush Theatre, London, and Manhattan Theatre Club, New York); *Elegy* (Donmar Warehouse, London; nominated for 2017 Olivier Award for Best New Play); *The Art of Dying* (Royal Court Theatre, London); *A Life* (Broadway and Public Theater; nominated for 2020 Tony Award for Best Play). Films include *The Sense of an Ending* and *We Live in Time*. Television includes *Wanderlust*.

by the same author from Faber

IF THERE IS I HAVEN'T FOUND IT YET
ONE DAY WHEN WE WERE YOUNG
WANDERLUST
CONSTELLATIONS
THE SAME DEEP WATER AS ME
INCOGNITO
ELEGY

NICK PAYNE

The Unbelievers

faber

First published in 2025
by Faber and Faber Limited
The Bindery, 51 Hatton Garden
London, EC1N 8HN

Typeset by Brighton Gray
Printed and bound in the UK by CPI Group (Ltd), Croydon CR0 4YY

All rights reserved
© Nick Payne, 2025

Nick Payne is hereby identified as author
of this work in accordance with Section 77 of the
Copyright, Designs and Patents Act 1988

All rights whatsoever in this work, amateur or professional,
are strictly reserved. Applications for permission for any use
whatsoever including performance rights must be made in
advance, prior to any such proposed use, to
Curtis Brown Group Ltd, Cunard House,
15 Regent Street, London SW1Y 4LR

No performance may be given unless a licence
has first been obtained

This book is sold subject to the condition that it shall not,
by way of trade or otherwise, be lent, resold, hired out
or otherwise circulated without the publisher's prior consent
in any form of binding or cover other than that in which
it is published and without a similar condition including
this condition being imposed on the subsequent purchaser

A CIP record for this book
is available from the British Library

ISBN 978-0-571-39902-4

Printed and bound in the UK on FSC® certified paper in line with our continuing
commitment to ethical business practices, sustainability and the environment.
For further information see faber.co.uk/environmental-policy

Our authorised representative in the EU for product safety is
Easy Access System Europe, Mustamäe tee 50, 10621 Tallinn, Estonia
gpsr.requests@easproject.com

2 4 6 8 10 9 7 5 3 1

The Unbelievers was first performed at the Royal Court Jerwood Theatre Downstairs on 10 October 2025, with the following cast:

PC Angela Fisher / Mia Olsson Isabel Adomakoh Young
Nancy Gomez Alby Baldwin
David Wright Paul Higgins
Margaret Wright Ella Lily Hyland
Benjamin Harry Kershaw
Karl Gomez Martin Marquez
PC Jay Shah / Anil Jaz Singh Deol
DC Elizabeth Hawkins / Lorraine Lucy Thackeray
Miriam Wright Nicola Walker

Director Marianne Elliott
Designer Bunny Christie
Lighting Designer Jack Knowles
Composer & Sound Designer Nicola T. Chang
Movement Director Etta Murfitt
Casting Director Charlotte Sutton CDG
Design Associate Verity Sadler
Assistant Director Anna Hampton
Props Supervisor Lily Mollgaard
Voice Coach Hazel Holder
Stage Manager Laura Draper
Deputy Stage Manager Surenee Somchit
Assistant Stage Manager Ava G. McCarthy

Acknowledgements

Adam Brace, Maggie Burrows, David Byrne (and everyone at the Royal Court Theatre), Jenny Cooper, Marianne Elliott, John Fraser, Thomas Kail, Missing People, G. L. Playfair, the Reverend Elisabeth Morse, Matthew Byam Shaw, Nick Sidi, Rebecca Taichman, Lily Williams and Minna always.

I would like to acknowledge the following books and their authors: *Faith, Hope and Carnage* by Nick Cave and Sean O'Hagan; *Conversations on Religion* edited by Mick Gordon and Chris Wilkinson; *Leaving Alexandria* by Richard Holloway; *Inventing the Universe* by Alister McGrath; *Ben* by Kerry Needham; *Time Lived, Without its Flow* by Denise Riley; *Spook* by Mary Roach; and *Paranormality* by Richard Wiseman. Lastly, I would like to acknowledge 'Puffins in Peril' by Mark Cocker, originally published in the *New Statesman*, 31 July 2016.

Characters

Miriam Wright
mid- to late forties or above

David Wright
mid- to late forties or above

Margaret Wright
seventeen at the time of Oscar's disappearance

Nancy Gomez
early twenties

Reverend Karl Gomez
mid- to late forties or above

DC Elizabeth Hawkins
family liaison officer, forties

PC Jay Shah
thirties or above

PC Angela Fisher
forties

Mia Olsson
early to mid-twenties

Anil
forties or above

Lorraine
late forties

Benjamin
thirties

THE UNBELIEVERS

For Adam Brace x

Notes

No blackouts, no scene changes and no transitions.

*

A change in formatting indicates a change in timeline:
The first week
One year later
Seven years later

This text went to press before the end of rehearsals and so may differ slightly from the play as performed.

Miriam's hand is wrapped in a scarf, dripping blood.

Miriam I went to Beverley.

David Beverley.

Miriam North of Hull.

Margaret You mean as in the place?

Miriam I had a message. About a sighting.

David In Beverley?

Miriam Trish and Dermot O'Reilly.

Margaret Why would he go to Beverley?

David Please tell me you called the police.

Miriam They sent me a DM. About a boy.

David Miriam. Please just at least tell me you –

Miriam Coming in and out of some record shop or other.

Margaret Why would he be at a record shop in Beverley?

Miriam They had this. Wall. Inside their – It looked like I mean I don't even know how many but as far as I could tell they had pretty much everything.

David I don't understand?

Miriam Coverage. Newspapers. Magazines. Online. Everything, floor to ceiling. That and a lot of stuff about UFOs.

David Jesus.

Margaret People are literally psychos.

Miriam They were extremely, and I really do mean extremely, convivial. Tea? No thanks. Sure, bit of cake, bit of fruit? All good. Battenberg?

Beat.

I asked about CCTV and the guy, I mean the guy behind the counter –

David This is the guy inside –

Miriam Inside the record shop, and he said, No – They're just dummies. The cameras, they don't, they're not – There's no actual, whatchamacallit.

David Feed?   Margaret Hard drive?

Miriam So Trish she showed him one of her many thousands of photographs.

David Showed the guy inside the record shop?

Margaret Of Oscar?

Miriam And he said – he said – he said – Teenagers these days they're all ten-a-penny.

Margaret I don't understand, what's 'ten-a-penny'?

David It's like –

Miriam It's means they're everywhere.

David Common.

Miriam Common?

David As in ubiquitous.

Miriam Ironically – And I know this because I googled it on the way home – the dictionary definition of 'ten-a-penny' is easy to find.

Margaret Grown men working in record shops are like a hundred per cent sexual predators.

This amuses Miriam.

Miriam Ha! We went across the street. To this place. Because it has all these windows. Directly overlooking the, you know, the shop –

David The record shop?

Miriam But it was one of these. You know. Places. Where the. Where they don't – What's-it-called – Theme. Themed.

David The couple from Beverley they took you to a themed restaurant –

Miriam You couldn't just order a sandwich. You had to have a waffle sandwich. You couldn't just order a burger – You had to order a waffle burger. They didn't do toasties – They only did waffle toasties.

Margaret So basically like waffles instead of bread.

Miriam We sat there staring out of that window for what felt like a fucking eternity.

Beat.

I went outside to throw up and then instead of going back inside I decided to head back to the B&B instead but I couldn't find my keys.

David Keys to the B&B you mean or you mean –

Miriam No to the car, car keys. I ended up having to use a gnome because my hand it was hurting so much from all the punching.

Margaret Wait –

David You're saying you broke into your own –

Miriam It was either that or throw myself off the Humber Bridge.

David She doesn't mean that. You don't mean that.

Miriam Don't I.

David Fuck's sake, Miriam – No. You don't. She doesn't.

Miriam All right all right all right. No. I don't. I'm sorry. Scout's honour. I don't. Honest. Honest. Cross my heart.

Margaret Can we see?

Miriam removes the scarf, it's bloody and gross under there.

David Jesus fucking Christ, Miriam.   Margaret Wow that is so fucked up.

Miriam I honestly think there's every chance it's nowhere near as bad as it looks.

Margaret It needs washing. I'm gonna go get the first-aid kit.

Margaret leaves the scene.

David Miriam look –

Miriam Kiss me.

David What?

Miriam I'm low on platelets, David, kiss me.

David I think that would be a mistake.

Miriam It doesn't have to be on the lips.

David Why don't I put the kettle on instead.

Miriam I won't tell anyone if you won't.

Beat. Margaret re-enters the scene with first-aid kit. Margaret proceeds to clean up Miriam's wound(s), with perhaps a little help from David. But mostly Margaret is the 'grown-up' here.

Margaret What were you guys talking about?

David I was telling Mum about the trip we went on at the weekend.

Margaret We went to a cathedral.

David Lorraine introduced us to the organist.

Miriam How is Lorraine?

David Yeah she's doing really well actually thank you.

Miriam Well that's good. That's good, I'm glad to hear it.

David She told us where the phrase 'all the stops', where it comes from.

Miriam Lorraine you mean or the –

Margaret I actually. Sorry.

Miriam What, what is it?

Margaret I'm not actually sure what I'm even s'posed to be doing.

Miriam Then stop. Mags, honestly it's fine don't worry about it.

Margaret No but what if it's broken?

Miriam Then I'll take some ibuprofen.

Margaret I think you need to see a doctor, Dad, I think she needs to see a doctor.

Miriam Relax. Please. Look.

Tries to move injured fingers, but clearly in pain.

All good.

Margaret All right I'm gonna go to bed.

David Night Mags. Sleep well.

David and Margaret embrace.

Margaret Night Mum.

Miriam Night Mags.

Margaret hesitates. Margaret moves to Miriam and hugs her, awkward. Margaret leaves the scene.

David Each pipe it has a knob.

Miriam What?

David Each pipe on the organ it has a knob.

Miriam A knob.

David A stop knob. And the organist, when they, if they pull out all of the stop knobs in simultaneity . . . in other words, when . . .

David . . . you pull out all of the stops . . .   Margaret . . . you pull out all the stops . . .

David . . . apparently you get this blast this wall of fucking sound.

Miriam kisses David, they savour it.

Miriam Did she do it for you?

David I mean. She was okay. But I was with Lorraine so I wasn't really in a position –

Miriam I meant did she play the fucking organ for you, David.

David No. She was pretty strict. She said we should come back another day. She said we should check out some Bach in the meantime. You like Bach?

Miriam I dunno. Sometimes.

David Tell me what should I be listening to, Bach-wise.

Miriam The cello suites, I dunno. Ask Nancy –

David I sent him an email, Miriam.

   Beat.

Miriam Martyn Oldfield you mean or you mean –

David What? No. Oscar.

Miriam Oh right yeah no I know.

David What –

Miriam David I log into his Gmail more or less every second of every day.

David I had no idea.

Miriam I've read all of the emails you've written to him.

David Wow that is so weird.

Miriam Is it? Why?

David I dunno for some reason it just feels weird to me, I feel weird about it.

Miriam Well don't.

She kisses him.

I like reading them.

She kisses him.

Some of the emails you've sent, David, they mean a lot.

She kisses him.

David So you saw the messages from Martyn?

Miriam Uh-huh.

They kiss.

David I mean the follow-up one, did you see the follow-up one?

Miriam Uh-huh.

They kiss.

I think we should do it. I don't see why we wouldn't.

They continue to kiss.

David Because the press are a bunch of fucking arseholes? Because they couldn't give less of a shit one way or the other what happens to us?

Miriam They're not all arseholes, David, that's not true. I like Martyn.

David I like Martyn too. But he works for *The Times*, Miriam, don't be naive.

Miriam I'm not. I just happen to think at this particular moment in time Martyn probably has a point. People have lost interest. The first anniversary is a milestone. We need more coverage. I like coverage. It makes me feel like something is actually happening.

David What about the trolls?

Miriam Fuck the trolls. Those creepy little bastards can go fuck 'emselves.

   Beat.

David Fuck you are so hot to me sometimes.

Miriam Are you sure we can't get you something else to drink?

Jay All good thanks.

Miriam Something to eat? Snack?

Jay All good.

Miriam Kit Kat?

   PC Angela Fisher enters the scene.

Angela Sorry about that. I had a bit of trouble with your – The flush on your – I tried –

Miriam It's been like that for a while, sorry I should have said.

David What d'you mean?

Miriam The flush on the downstairs loo it's broken.

David Why didn't you tell me – I would've –

Margaret Dad.

David No but how long is 'a while', I would've –

Margaret It is literally making no difference to anyone's existence.

David What about the upstairs loo is everything all right with the loo upstairs?

Beat.

Miriam Where were we?

Angela We were talking about –

Jay Oscar's upcoming –

Angela Birthday.

Miriam His sixteenth. He's going to be sixteen.

Margaret In a coupla weeks.

Jay In a couple of weeks' time, that's right.

Beat.

Also you mentioned a . . . dinner?

Miriam Sunday evening. We all had dinner together here Sunday evening.

Angela Everyone here was at dinner?

Miriam Yes.   **David** Yeah.

Nancy Plus my girlfriend. Ellen. Ellen Holloway.

Angela How was it?

Flicker of hesitation.

Margaret Dad and Ellen had a row 'cause not only is Ellen Christian she's also, like, consumed by veganism.

Nancy They were meeting for the first time. Also Ellen was brought up Christian but I wouldn't necessarily say like –

Margaret (*on 'Also'*) Dad hates vegans.

David Come on – That's not – I don't –

Margaret And Mum and Dad're both like raging atheists.

David I do not 'hate vegans' –

Miriam It wasn't a particularly light-hearted meal, no, but as healthy disagreements go, I think Oscar's seen worse.

Angela What sort of things did you talk about? Over dinner.

Miriam Well. We talked about . . .

David Nancy and Ellen are studying together – We talked about that. It's hard to say exactly; it wasn't a particularly memorable evening.

Nancy Oh I'm sorry, were we –

David I didn't mean –

Miriam We talked about God. Michael Schumacher. ABBA. Evander Holyfield. *Home Alone*. Climate change.

Nancy The Jackson Five.

David Albumen.

Jay Was Oscar part of the conversation?

Miriam Yes very much so.   **Nancy** Yeah for sure.   **Margaret** Definitely.

Angela And yesterday, yesterday morning I mean –

Miriam What about it?

Jay Uh-huh.

Nancy Did we see him d'you mean?

Angela Yes.

Nancy I was asleep.

Miriam We saw each other and everything seemed fine and he said goodbye.

Angela Margaret?

Margaret We normally get the same bus, but him and his mates they watched some like weird documentary recently about hiking, so they decided to start walking to school instead.

Jay So he didn't seem, I dunno, there didn't seem to be anything about him that was, like, out of the ordinary –

Miriam No it was ordinary, it was all ordinary, the whole morning was ordinary. We had breakfast and we said goodbye.

Margaret Yeah I'd probably say like, yeah like, ordinary yeah.

Nancy He sent me a link to this video actually.

Miriam What do you mean?

Nancy During the day, sorry, he sent me a link to this video . . .

David What did it say?

Nancy There wasn't any text, there was just the link.

Angela Did you follow the link?   **Jay** And did you follow the link?

Nancy Yeah it was a video of a slow loris.

Angela A slow . . . ?

Nancy It's a bit like a . . . How specific d'you need me to be?

Angela As much as you feel . . .

Jay It's all beneficial.

Nancy They're like cats but with really big eyes. And in the video someone's tickling the slow loris and its arms are in the air and its head is tilted back like it's having the time of its life. And then when the person stops tickling, the slow loris slowly lowers its arms and it looks like totally heartbroken. The slow loris wants the tickling to continue I guess is what we're s'posed to infer.

Jay Gotcha.

Angela What time did you receive the message with the link?

Nancy Not sure, but I can check.

Nancy takes out their phone and checks during the following.

Miriam Also.

Jay Please.

Miriam I'm not sure how relevant this is – But Oscar had recently had braces fitted, and a week or so ago we did have a very brief conversation about some boys who had been teasing him. Because of his braces.

Nancy (*re time link was received*) Twelve thirty-seven.

David What?

Miriam I don't think it was necessarily anything particularly –

David This is the first I've heard?

Angela We can check with the school.

David Hang on –

Miriam I don't imagine they'll know anything about it –

David You're saying he was being bullied?

Miriam No, I think really all I'm saying is that there had been some kind of isolated incident involving one or two boys teasing Oscar about his braces. Also. He has an ingrowing toenail.

David (*on 'Also'*) Why didn't you tell me?

Jay Oh okay.

Miriam And he'd been planning a skating trip to Folkestone with some of his closest friends.

David Folkestone, really?

Miriam Folkestone 51.

Angela You seem surprised?

David considers his response.

Margaret Dad's not living here.

David Mags, Jesus.

Margaret What? It is literally gonna come up in like two questions' time.

Nancy She's right.

Miriam It's okay – It's all right. She's right. It's true. We're separating.

Margaret (*on 'We're'*) They're getting divorced.

Angela And how, uhm, long has it, erm, been the case that –

Miriam A month.

David I moved out a month or so ago. Maybe less. Most of my belongings are still here, give or take.

Miriam It's a process. Ongoing.

Jay How aware was Oscar?

Miriam He knew everything there was to know. We talked him through everything.

Beat.

Angela It sounds like there have been quite a lot of moving parts at home recently.

Miriam I think that would be a fair assessment, yes.

Jay How does Oscar normally get home from school?

Margaret We get the bus.

Angela Together?

Margaret We don't technically like get it together because we're in different years but yeah it's the same bus.

Angela And when did you notice Oscar wasn't on the bus?

Margaret I guess the thing is it's like – It's normally pretty full for the first like five, six stops and then when it starts to thin out, that's normally when I see him sitting at the back with all his mates.

Jay And Oscar was or wasn't on the bus?

Margaret Wasn't.

Angela When you realised Oscar wasn't present, did you, what did you do?

Margaret (*shrugs, perhaps*) I guess because of the whole walking-hiking thing it's like – Sometimes he just pretty habitually does his own thing.

Angela And what about, what time are you normally home, Miriam?

Miriam Unless I'm held up, I'll normally make it home between six and seven – If not a bit earlier. Seven at the absolute latest.

Angela flicks through her notebook for the exact time.

Angela And you contacted emergency services –

Miriam I think it was about ten to ten.

Angela And before that –

Miriam I called his friends, I mean his friends' parents, I called them. I called the school, I mean they were closed obviously but I thought it might be worth a try. I called the library, the library down the road he sometimes goes to. I mean everybody, neighbours, friends, I called his piano teacher, fish and chip place, the chicken shop.

David We've been up and down the street.

Jay What about any other family nearby?

Miriam We don't –

David We don't really have any other family nearby. Most of them live in the sticks.

Miriam They don't live in the – What he means is they don't live in the city.

David Come on, to get to your aunt's place we have to hike –

Nancy There's my dad? I dunno, is that – Karl. Karl Gomez.

Jay Right.   **Angela** Oh okay.

Nancy Obviously he's not strictly speaking related to Oscar, but.

Angela I'm sorry I think I'm slightly – Karl Gomez is –

Nancy Mum's first husband my dad, yeah.

Jay Gotcha.

David But he's not Oscar's father, I'm Oscar's –

Miriam He lives on the other side of the city. Karl.

Jay It might be useful to have his address, contact number as well?

Miriam Absolutely.

Angela Likewise address and contact details of any friends, best friends –

Miriam Absolutely –

Angela Anyone really you think Oscar might –

Miriam Definitely.

Jay We'll also need a recent photo –

Miriam Would you like those now, or –

Jay No I think let's –

Angela We can get to all of that in a moment. You all mentioned earlier you tried calling Oscar –

David Yeah, no.   **Miriam** His mobile.

Angela And did the phone ring, or were you –

Miriam It went straight to voicemail.   **David** Straight to voicemail.

Miriam Text message. WhatsApp. Nothing.

Jay Does . . . Oscar use Facebook?

Miriam No. Facebook is for old people.

Angela What about social media in general?

David He's on his phone all the time.   **Miriam** I'd say his favourites are probably Instagram and Snapchat.

Nancy YouTube.   **Margaret** YouTube.

Jay Do you know any of his usernames and or passwords?

Miriam All of them, yes.

Jay It would be great to get those as well.

David No. (*Reacting to Miriam's 'All of them'.*) Wow, really?

Angela What about access to money; does Oscar have a debit or credit card?

Miriam He has an account with HSBC.

David He has an account with HSBC.

David Sorry.

Miriam No.

David You go . . .

Miriam I was just gonna say he hasn't used it. We have an app.

Jay Be great to get the details on that as well.

Miriam Absolutely.   **David** Course.

Angela Have you noticed anything missing from the house?

David Missing?

Miriam No. Nothing is missing.

Jay Lastly.

Angela Has Oscar ever gone missing before?

Miriam No. Never.

David *I'd like to organise a memorial.*

Miriam *A what?*

David *A memorial.*

Miriam *Meaning what exactly?*

David *A service. For Oscar.*

Miriam *You mean funeral?*

David *No –*

Miriam *You mean you want to organise a funeral?*

David *No what I'm saying is the – Maybe vigil is a better way of –*

Miriam *In a church?*

David *Maybe.*

Miriam *Why in a church?*

David *Because – It's complicated – I don't know! – I think it might do an awful lot of people an awful lot of good.*

Miriam *Who're these awful lots of people?*

David *Friends, family – You and I aren't the only ones who've been affected, Miriam –*

Miriam *D'you want hymns, are we talking hymns?*

David *I would be interested in having a – At a later stage, when we're both a little –*

Miriam *Do you or do you not want hymns, David?*

David *Yeah. I think so. Yeah I like hymns. What's wrong with singing some hymns?*

Miriam *And prayers?*

David *Miriam – I don't – How can I –*

Karl *I think what David is maybe tryina say –*

Miriam *I want David to know what David's trying to say thanks.*

David *Yes – Most likely – Yes – There would be a prayer.*

Miriam *A prayer for Oscar?*

David *Maybe.*

  Beat.

It's been seven years, Miriam, seven –

Miriam *Sorry, you don't have any chewing gum on you do you?*

David *What?*

Miriam *Chewing gum.*

David rummages in pocket, offers chewing gum to Miriam –

No not me, you.

David *What?*

Miriam *I'm just saying, I'm finding it incredibly hard to concentrate –*

David *Jesus fucking Christ, Miriam –*

Karl *Okay, all right –*

David *Fuck is wrong with you?*

Miriam *It's a distracting odour, don't take it so personally, Jesus –*

David *I know you know as well as I do, that seven years means we have the right to apply for a certificate of presumed death. Now I'm not saying that is something I want to do –*

Miriam *Good –*

David *That is not what I'm saying –*

Miriam *Glad to fucking hear it.*

David *But what I am saying is it is a marker. You know? Milestone moment. And it got me thinking. Perhaps we shouldn't just let it pass by unnoticed.*

Beat.

Miriam *Who else have you spoken to about this?*

David *Only Mags.*

Miriam *And Karl.*

David *Well evidently yeah I've also spoken to Karl about this.*

Miriam *(to Karl)* What do you think?

Karl *Look. I'm only really here as a –*

Miriam *We all know why you're here, Karl, you're here to make sure I don't go apeshit and start –*

Karl *I don't think a decision needs to be reached right away, that's what I think. It's about hearing everyone out. Space. But since you're asking.*

Miriam *Uh-huh.*

Karl *Since you're asking.*

Miriam *Yep.*

Karl *I think you've been through a hell of a lot. Separately as well as together. And I think that acknowledging that. Publicly. You know, in whatever way, whatever form. I think yeah, I think acknowledging that amongst a congregation of friends, family, I can see a world where something if not beneficial than maybe at the very least productive, is gonna come your way as a result of doing so.*

Miriam *What did Mags say?*

David *She said she would support our decision.*

Miriam *No she – Those were her exact words were they?*

David *Obviously they – I don't keep a written record of every –*

Miriam *All right – All right – Sorry. That was snide.*

David *It was snide.*

Miriam *I said it was snide.*

David *And I'm saying thank you for acknowledging that you were being snide.*

Beat.

Miriam I promise you I am not trying to –

Miriam *Why do you want to do it, David, that's what I don't understand? What would be the –*

David *Solace. Comfort. I don't know. Hope?*

Miriam smirks, maybe laughs.

Don't fucking laugh at me, Miriam.

Miriam *I wasn't –*

David *Mags told me what happened in the supermarket you know.*

Beat.

She told me you screamed at some poor stranger in the supermarket because – I don't know – she pushed in front of you?

Miriam *That wasn't what – Why are you dredging up something that happened –*

David *She told me you called her from the supermarket – Sobbing.*

Miriam *I . . .*

David *She's not coming back here, Miriam. When she graduates. She finds it incredibly hard.*

Miriam *What d'you mean? She said that to you?*

Karl *I wonder if we're veering a little off the beaten –*

Miriam *I don't believe she said that to you.*

David *Well I'm telling you she did.*

Beat.

She loves you Miriam, but equally I think she misses the person you were before.

Miriam *Fuck's that supposed to mean?*

David *It means sometimes I think she feels a little overlooked.*

Miriam How much was the taxi?

Nancy It doesn't matter.

Miriam Let me give you some money.

Margaret Mum it doesn't matter.

Miriam How much was it?

Margaret Mum!

Beat.

Miriam You should have called. I would have come to pick you up.

Nancy Yeah well it was kind of impromptu.

Miriam Why, what happened?

Nancy hesitates.

Margaret Mum and Dad had sex.

Nancy What? When?

Miriam Margaret –

Margaret Like last week.

Nancy When you say Dad you mean –

Margaret Mum was like three hours late to pick me up cause she went to Beverley.

Nancy Beverley?

Miriam Can we –

Margaret As in the place.

Nancy I don't understand?

Margaret Mum had a DM about a sighting in Beverley –

Nancy Fuck would he be doing in Beverley?

Miriam Look –

Margaret Well exactly, it's like, fuck would anybody be doing in Beverley?

Miriam All right –

Margaret She smashed up her hand.

Nancy What?

Miriam Excuse me –

Margaret She literally broke into her own car using her actual fist.

Nancy Wait. Fuck does smashing up your hand in Beverley have to do with sleeping with your ex –

Margaret (*on 'Fuck'*) And a gnome. Fist and gnome.

Miriam None of your business!

Nancy It's a little bit our business, no?

Miriam If you really –

Nancy I mean in so far as we just wanna know you're all right.

Miriam Why is my being sexually active somehow indicative –

Nancy Because, Mum, hate-fucking your ex is like basically self-harm.

Margaret Bold.

Miriam LOOK: I was in a tremendous, tremendous amount of pain feeling tremendously, tremendously sorry for myself –

Nancy It's just such a fucking cliché, Mum, ugh my God!

Miriam Yeah well you know what else is a cliché – Showing up, unannounced, without any kind of explanation in advance whatsoever –

Nancy Yeah you're right, sleeping with your ex and showing up at your actual mother's home, they're like basically the same thing –

Miriam You still haven't answered any of my questions, Nancy.

Nancy Ugh – All right! – Fine!

Beat.

There were these like. Calls. These like weird calls. To my phone.

Margaret How weird are we talking?   Miriam I don't understand?

Nancy As in, there would be the call, I would answer, and then there would just be nothing.

Margaret Wait. What?   Miriam When you say 'nothing' –

Nancy No one would be on the other end of the line.

Miriam So somebody was calling you but nobody was there?   Margaret As in like someone was pranking you?

Nancy I don't know how to explain it . . .

Miriam Or someone from the press?

Margaret Why would the press be all like breathy and weird?

Nancy Basically there was this one night, and I'd been out, I'd been out and I'd gotten like somewhat heinously wasted –

Margaret – Classic –

Nancy – and it was like the same thing all over again. Unknown number, silence on the other end of the line. So I like. Tossed it into the canal.

Margaret The phone?

Nancy The phone.

Margaret You were just like: I am *done* with this shit –

Nancy Totally, but then, yeah, later on, when Ellen was tryina get a hold of me – And by the time I'd gotten back to the flat, the rain was torrential and Ellen was like, I mean she unleashed what I suspect looking back on it was a fairly legitimate tirade –

Margaret Like what?

Nancy Well. As in. I don't understand why you're behaving this way. You've been behaving really erratically recently. You're unreliable.

Miriam In what sense unreliable?

Nancy She said maybe I ought to try speaking to someone again because maybe the anniversary of Oscar's disappearance is really fucking me up.

Margaret What did you say?

Nancy I said I've had enough therapy to sink a fucking ship, thank you very much, so how about you go fuck yourself –

Margaret No way did you say –

Nancy And then I started crying and I told her how much I love her. How much she means to me. How much being with her saved me.

Margaret What'd she say?

Nancy She just stared at me.

Beat.

Margaret What's the status with the phone?

Nancy Got a new one.

Margaret Let's see.

Nancy shows Margaret her new phone.

Nice.

Miriam Nancy, what does 'somewhat heinously wasted' mean?

Nancy What?

Beat.

It means I was having a shit time and I felt like letting off some steam.

Miriam Right.

Beat.

Nancy Mum it was nothing.

Miriam Doesn't sound like nothing.

Beat.

What about talking to somebody?

Nancy What about it?

Miriam Would you consider doing it again?

Nancy Would you?

Beat.

Miriam Well I'm sorry.

Beat.

We liked Ellen.

Beat.

You should have called. I would have come to pick you up.

Beat.

Why don't we get these bags upstairs.

Miriam leaves the scene (with bags if there are any).

Margaret You know that autistic kid?

Nancy You mean Chris?

Margaret Yeah he's always screaming.

Nancy His name is Chris, Mags.

Margaret Yeah she ran over his bike.

Nancy You mean Mum?

Margaret She fucking drove over it. Like properly *properly* – Back and forth.

Nancy You're kidding?

Margaret People were coming out of their fucking *houses*. The whole street. And Chris starts bawling his fucking eyes out.

Nancy Wait, this is before or after the thing in Beverley?

Margaret This is yesterday. Rob, you know the guy with the leaf blower, he tries to convince Mum to get out of the car and she tells him to go fuck himself.

Beat.

All I'm tryina say is I think it's been getting worse.

Margaret is growing upset.

And it's like. Yeah. I dunno. It's like. I dunno what I'm s'posed to be doing anymore.

Margaret is growing upset. Nancy gives Margaret a hug.

I really miss having you around, Nance.

The hug continues.

Nancy David is such a prick.

Margaret He is like technically still my dad, Nanc.

Nancy That's why it's important you know he's a prick.

Miriam Are you sure we can't get you something to drink, Elizabeth?

Elizabeth No thank you.

Miriam Something to eat? Snack?

Elizabeth I'm good, thank you.

Miriam Dime bar?

Margaret Mum – **Nancy** Mum –

Miriam Sorry – Sorry – I'm just a bit – It's just all a bit –

Elizabeth Don't apologise.

Miriam It's just a lot.

Elizabeth It absolutely is.

Miriam I haven't slept.

Elizabeth I'm sorry to hear that.

Miriam And I'm fucking clucking for a drink. I mean, fucking, clucking. There, I said it.

Beat.

Anyway sorry I interrupted, you were saying . . .

Elizabeth Not a problem. That's right. There are several strands to the investigation.

Miriam Okay.

Elizabeth House-to-house –

Miriam House-to-house?

Elizabeth Yes.

Miriam Knocking on doors?

Elizabeth That's right.

Miriam Knocking on doors and talking to people?

Elizabeth That's right.

Miriam Asking them if they've seen or, or, or, you know, what's-the-fucking –

David Heard.

Miriam Heard. Asking them if they've seen or heard, fucking – Because we've been doing that.

Elizabeth I understand.

Miriam We've been doing that – I mean we have been there, done that –

Margaret Mum.	**Nancy** Mum.
David Look it's okay, it's all right –	**Miriam** It's important – I'm just saying it's important. Because we have been doing that. Already. For days.

Elizabeth I'm sure.

Miriam We've been doing that, all of us, for days.

Elizabeth I'm sure. I understand. We will be going house-to-house potentially across quite a wide perimeter.

David Around the school presumably?

Elizabeth That will include around the school, absolutely.

Miriam And how is that – Sorry, just so I understand – How is that any different from what the four of us have been doing?

Elizabeth Well. Truthfully. Depending on who is at the door, you know, depending upon who is now asking the questions, people might simply react a little differently.

Miriam You mean if they don't have some mad woman screaming at them.

Elizabeth It also in truth, it sends a very clear message to the local community that this is serious. This is real now. It raises the profile of the investigation. People, perhaps, possibly, might be a little more willing to share, say, something, that they might not have been, perhaps felt able to share with, say, one of you – Also memory is a fickle business. Memories come, memories go. Sometimes, with a little time passing, with a little careful prodding, guess what, all of a sudden people remember. They see the scale, the severity of the investigation being undertaken and all of a sudden a memory is jogged. A memory is jogged, a witness statement is taken, and now all of a sudden we have a new line of enquiry to pursue. Is everything that I'm saying making sense to you all?

Everybody nods affirmative.

We will also be interviewing teachers and pupils at the school, as well as gathering CCTV footage, carrying out local searches, gathering as much digital data, forensics, as we possibly can. The investigation will also more than likely be in contact with the UK Missing Persons Unit, that's the national point of contact for all missing persons investigations. And at some point, I'd also like to spend a little time speaking to each of you individually.

Miriam Absolutely. Whatever you need.

Margaret How come?

Elizabeth (*to Margaret*) Well, again, it's so that we can have a sense of Oscar – Build up a – His habits, his routines –

Margaret No, okay.

Elizabeth The preference, or perhaps the goal rather, at this stage, is to ascertain as *much* as we can, as *close* as we can, to the disappearance itself.

David What are the statistics? Sorry.

Elizabeth No, ask away. The statistics, you mean . . . ?

David How many, yeah, people are – found – How many are – I dunno – How many're –

Elizabeth I have never personally been involved in a missing persons investigation in which the missing person has – The majority of missing persons, particularly within this age range, are runaways.

David Really?

Elizabeth That's right.

Nancy Have you ever had to stop?

David Stop? **Margaret** Why would you stop?

Elizabeth Well. Look. It's a good question. A missing persons investigation is always open, remains open, but whether or not the investigation remains *active* will depend upon, somewhat broadly speaking, length of time versus accumulation of evidence.

Beat.

Miriam What else can we do? To help.

Elizabeth Well, at some point, as and when you have a moment, it's not pressing, but at some point we'll need to take a swab from the two of you. (*Meaning Miriam and David.*)

Miriam Absolutely.   **David** A swab?

Elizabeth From the inside of your mouths.

David What for?

Elizabeth Identification.

Margaret Identification of what?

Beat.

Miriam And is that. Is that. Is that something you need to – Do you want to do that now? Or . . .

Elizabeth No. We can do that tomorrow. Or, as I say, as and when . . . There's no per se rush at this stage.

David Where is he – on the . . . Risk – I don't know what it's – Spectrum? – I don't know what to call it?

Elizabeth This is high-risk.

David Really?

Elizabeth That's right.

David Why, what makes it high-risk?

Miriam Under sixteen.   **Elizabeth** Being under sixteen –

David Really? Wow, I didn't realise –

Elizabeth Being under sixteen –

David So this is pretty serious?

| **Nancy** Obviously. | **Miriam** Jesus David in what universe – | **David** (*on 'in'*) With – I'm talking about – Within the framework of the – |

Elizabeth We're taking this very seriously indeed, yes.

Miriam *Why are you holding a banana skin?*

Margaret *I couldn't find a bin.*

Miriam *How long have you been carrying it around for?*

Margaret *What?*

Miriam *How long have –*

Margaret *No I meant what, as in why is this a thing you're talking to me about?*

Miriam *It's unhygienic.*

Margaret *Excuse me for tryina save the fucking planet.*

Miriam *One banana skin isn't going to save the planet.*

Margaret *Is this for real – Are you really – This is such a –*

Miriam *Your father came to see me.*

Beat.

He said to me the two of you had spoken on the phone?

Margaret *He called me, I didn't –*

Miriam *You told him about the supermarket –*

Margaret *Look –*

Miriam *You told him about what happened in the supermarket?*

Margaret *I did, but –*

Miriam *He said you want to have a memorial.*

Margaret *Well that is not at all what I said, so –*

Miriam *Fuck did you tell him about the supermarket for?*

Margaret *Because sometimes you're a fucking lunatic and I get worried about you.*

Miriam *If you don't want me to call you –*

Margaret *Of course I want you to call me – Don't you dare stop calling me, 'cause I t—*

Miriam *Why do you want a memorial?*

Margaret *I don't.*

Miriam *That's not what your father said to me.*

Margaret *I said to him – I said I theoretically see nothing wrong with the two of you having a conversation about some kind of event for Oscar.*

Miriam *Hymns?*

Margaret *What?*

Miriam *Where do you stand on hymns?*

Margaret *I am literally not prepared to get caught in the middle of some –*

Miriam *He said you're not going to come home once you graduate.*

   Beat.

Margaret *I. He shouldn't have told you that –*

Miriam *So it's true?*

Margaret *Listen if I decide not to come home, it isn't because of anything you've done.*

Miriam *I don't believe you.*

Margaret *All right fine, me not coming home might potentially have something to do with the, like, most recent spate of mental episodes –*

Miriam *What d'you mean, like what?*

Margaret *I'm not prepared to list your mental episodes.*

Miriam *I honestly would like your perspective.*

Margaret *Fuck. I wanna see you and I wanna spend time with you. But sometimes it's like, the only thing that's going on inside my head is like, is she about to go mental? Is this another thing she's gonna go mental about? And specifically on the whole coming home thing. I guess it's, like. His room. The fact that you still have it. That it's so clean. The fact that you clean it, like, literally religiously –*

Miriam *It's important to preserve any evidence.*

Margaret *My room needs hoovering, why don't you hoover my room?*

Beat.

Also. I mean I guess like the main reason.

Beat.

Are you all right?

Miriam *I'm fine.*

Margaret *You're allowed to say no.*

Miriam *I said I'm fine.*

Margaret *You asked for my perspective!*

Beat.

Okay, so you remember I told you about Benjamin?

Miriam *What?*

Margaret *Benjamin. He works for the JNCC.*

Miriam *Vaguely.*

Margaret *Joint Nature Conservation Committee. We met at the lido.*

Miriam *Okay.*

Margaret *I showed you his fucking picture!*

Miriam *Oh you mean the old guy?*

Margaret *What?*

Miriam *I remember –*

Margaret *He's thirty-fucking-seven!*

Miriam *Older than you I mean – He's older than –*

Margaret *You're so retrograde sometimes –*

Miriam *I'm not saying it's a big deal, I'm just saying it's worthy of note –*

Margaret *Well you're a fucking idiot because this was s'posed to be like – But fine, fuck it, it's like who gives a shit anyway . . .*

Margaret passes her smartphone to Miriam.

That's from an ultrasound like four days ago.

Miriam *I don't understand?*

Margaret YOU'RE LOOKING AT A PHOTOGRAPH OF THE INSIDE OF MY WOMB.

Miriam *No I understand that bit. That bit I understand. It's the bit about the man I'm struggling with.*

Margaret *You mean Benjamin.*

Miriam *Benjamin. From the lido.*

Margaret *The lido is just where we met, it's not some like great –*

Miriam *And you met, at the lido, and you thought to yourselves –*

Margaret *Six months ago. We met six fucking months ago, Mum –*

Miriam *Okay and so after six months the two of you, you thought to yourselves, you thought: I know. What would be good. Right now. At such a young age. At such an early stage –*

Margaret *You're horrible. D'you know that? You're literally –*

Miriam *I'm just trying to ascertain the degree to which – Because it's a lot. A child is a tremendous, tremendous responsibility, Margaret –*

Margaret *Oh my God, d'you know something, you're right. We've barely thought this through. Oh my God, what a couple of absolute morons –*

Miriam *That's not what I'm saying. Margaret. Please –*

Margaret *No, d'you know what – Forget it. Forget it. Fuck.*

Beat.

When I told Dad he was like genuinely delighted. FYI.

Miriam *Good.*

Margaret *Lorraine gave me an actual hug.*

Miriam *Margaret, if you're looking for a hug all you have to –*

Margaret *I'm not some fucking child.*

Miriam *I know. I know you're not.*

Margaret *I know what I'm doing.*

Miriam *Good. I'm glad.*

Margaret *Anyway Dad wants to get everyone together to celebrate.*

Anil has an A4 document wallet. Mia takes notes as Nancy speaks.

Miriam Are you sure we can't get you something to drink, either of you?

Anil Not for me thank you.

Mia All good.

Miriam Something to eat? Snack?

Anil I'm good, thank you.

Mia I literally just ate.

Miriam Wagon Wheel?

Nancy Mum.

Anil Oh wow. Blast from the past.

Awkward beat.

Well. Miriam. Nancy. We thank you. Again. For contacting the Society. Regarding your recent. Experiences.

Nancy Thanks for getting back to us.

Anil Oh definitely, for sure.

Beat.

Well. There really is no set format or formula that we need to adhere to. In terms of – Some people. For example. Find it preferable to jump right in. Alternatively, on the other hand. I can tell you a little bit more about myself, my background, my role as Chair of the Society's Spontaneous Cases Committee.

Nancy Sounds great, yeah. Jumping right in I mean.

Anil Okay. Great. Well.

Nancy Not quite sure where to start.

Anil No. Well. That's okay.

Beat, checks his notes, then:

Well, we have your original submission. Regarding a series of telephone calls from an unknown number.

Nancy Uh-huh, yeah.

Anil And then in your follow-up correspondences with the Society, and also during my conversation with you Miriam, there was mention of a possible anomalous experience.

Mia Possible apparition?

Nancy Yeah. Well, so, I was asleep. I'd been sleeping. And I felt this draught. So I figured there must be a window open –

Just then Anil's smartphone rings. Anil hurries to retrieve smartphone from pocket.

Anil I'm so sorry – Please accept my –

Miriam There's really no need to apologise.

Nancy It's honestly – It's totally fine.

Anil 'rejects' the call.

Anil Apologies. Where were we?

Nancy . . .

Mia You were saying you'd felt a draught. You were saying you figured there must a window open . . .

Nancy Oh yeah except there wasn't.

Mia Wasn't a window open or wasn't a draught?

Nancy Both. Actually. Windows were locked and so then it was like. Yeah I dunno. It's weird I s'pose don't exactly know how to . . .

Anil Take your time.

Nancy I s'pose when I realised it wasn't a draught, it was like . . . I realised it was a bit like a presence? Or something?

Just then Anil's smartphone rings. Anil hurries to retrieve smartphone from pocket.

Anil Oh my gosh – I am so, so sorry –

Mia Maybe put it on airplane mode to be on the safe side?

Miriam Don't apologise please.

Nancy It's honestly like – If you need to take the call you should take the call.

Anil You know what, I might just send her a quick . . .

Miriam Good idea, Anil. **Nancy** Totally.

Anil texts, awkward beat.

Anil Great. Good. Sorry. Thank you. Now where were we –

Mia A draught, a bit like a presence, or something.

Nancy Yeah, no. As in. All of a sudden it felt a bit like someone else was in the room with me.

Mia Felt a bit like someone else was in the room with you.

Nancy Yeah, no – As in – Yeah. As in, all of a sudden, that was how it felt.

Mia Wow.

Nancy But it wasn't – I dunno. It's like. Fuck I dunno how to . . .

Mia It's okay, take your time.

Nancy I guess I would say that like overall – In terms of the overall experience, it was more like weird than frightening. As in it wasn't necessarily like this massively frightening – It was just like. Holy shit: I think there might be somebody else in here.

Mia Totally.

Nancy And maybe I should probably say, I'm studying at LIPA, so I'm not here a lot of the time, so my old room has become like a kind of spare room?

Mia What're you studying?

Nancy Music.

Mia No way, that's so cool. Do you write your own stuff?

Nancy Yeah trying to.

Mia What d'you play?

Nancy Um, piano. Guitar. Bass if there's an emergency.

Mia When was the last time you found yourself in the middle of a bass emergency?

Nancy Yeah fair point.

They might be smiling, they might have laughed a little.

Anyway –

Mia 'Nurse we're losing him, we need some bass, stat'!

Beat.

Nancy The piano in the room is the piano my brother used to practise on. And so then it was like, yeah, a couple of nights later, same sort of thing sort of happened again? A draught. A presence. An outline. Beside the piano. So I tried turning on the light – Not the main light, just the light beside my bed. Except it didn't work. It wasn't working. So I got out of bed. As in tried to move a little closer. And when I got closer it was like. I dunno. The outline or whatever the fuck, it was like. It was like a boy. Not like a really little kid. But a boy. And so then I dunno I waved. Said hi. Hello, I said. And then fuck it I dunno I turned on the light, the main light, I dunno. And then I. Yeah. Started crying. Mum came in. Room was empty.

Beat.

What d'you think?

Anil Well. The Society first and foremost is a scientific organisation –

Nancy Do you think I sound like an insane person?

Anil No. No I do not. I don't think that at all. In fact listening to you speak, Nancy, I'm reminded of the importance of not hurrying toward convenient or snap conclusions.

Nancy I don't understand?

Anil Well. I think in the first instance. We ought to consider any possible physical and psychological factors potentially at play here. For example. Sleep. Stress. Mental health –

Nancy Sorry sorry – I – I still don't understand?

Anil Well. There are organisations and or groups out there, Nancy, that would certainly rush to define the experiences you describe as inexplicable – Or at the very least beyond the reach of science for sure. However at the Society by-and-large we favour a more rigorous approach. Certainly I feel a duty of care in the first instance to eliminate each and every possible entirely explicable explanation.

Nancy So you do think I sound like an insane person . . .	Anil And of course when we reach the point where science is no longer able to provide us with a compelling explanation –

Nancy So you guys are like ghost-hunters who don't believe in actual ghosts?

Anil Well. We're academics. My particular interest is in paranormal beliefs and their relationship to personality and cognition. And so in no small part I joined the Society in order to test the outer limits of my own scepticism. And certainly what I've found –

Nancy So you think science called my fucking phone and said nothing? You think *science* put a fucking boy inside my bedroom –

Miriam All right –

Nancy No but it's like – Fuck even is this?

Mia For what it's worth I'm like an out-and-out believer. Hundred per cent. And I've been on visits with some of the like, full-on amateur ghost-hunting dudes – And honestly the thing that sets the Society apart – Is that it's like this insanely broad open-minded methodical church. The Society's annual conference is like a straight-up banger. And so yeah I guess maybe what Anil's tryina get at –

Anil (*on 'visits'*) I really didn't mean to cause any offence, Nancy. I believe there is help we can offer. Perhaps my struggle is somewhat of an ethical one here . . .

Nancy I guess I just I dunno how much longer I can handle feeling like this.

Mia Totally.

Anil No. I can only begin to imagine.

Beat.

Anil The human brain is a meaning-seeking device, Nancy. For better and sometimes for worse. Our beliefs and our experiences they do not sit placidly inside our brains. Quite the opposite. Often our minds they are shaping our experience of the world around us. Which is why in this particular instance –

Just then Anil's smartphone rings.

I'm so – Please accept my –

He takes the call.

Jane? Jane? I sent you a – I'm in the middle –

Anil checks his phone, battery has died, shut down.

Unbelievable. (*To Miriam.*) I'm so sorry to have to ask but I don't suppose you might happen to have a charger I –

Miriam Of course.

Anil It might be better to try and just, nip this one in the bud, for want of a better –

Miriam You can always just use the landline if you like. The signal round here can be pretty useless.

Anil Who doesn't love a landline.

Anil and Miriam leave the scene. Beat.

Mia Can I suggest something possibly a little inappropriate?

Beat.

Can I give you my number?

Nancy Uh – I'm – I recently broken up with someone, so –

Mia No – Shit – Sorry – Not for romantic purposes –

Nancy Fuck, ah, okay.

Mia No, but –

Nancy That was embarrassing –

Mia No but here's the thing though – You are like definitely –

Nancy It's okay, you don't need to –

Mia No but listen because – I would love that. I would. To talk. More. About your experiences –

Nancy It's honestly fine, you don't –

Mia I'm not asking.

Mia rummages in her pockets, and writes down her telephone number on a piece of paper. Mia passes piece of paper to Nancy. Beat.

Nancy So how long have you been with the Spontaneous Cases Committee?

Mia Oh I'm not.

Nancy I don't understand?

Mia I'm doing a BSc in Psychology? My main area of interest is our interaction with paranormal events – Belief and the paranormal. And so my supervisor put me in touch with Anil back in like – And 'cause Anil's so cool he basically said it would be cool for me – And so when your enquiry came in, full disclosure, I pretty much begged Anil to let me – So I s'pose I'm sort of moonlighting? Essentially? But I am a member of the Society. Just to be clear.

Nancy Oh okay.

Mia It is pretty fucking sexy stuff, I don't mind telling you.

Beat.

It's not really, I don't know why I say stuff like that.

Beat.

I'm really sorry about your brother, Nancy. I know it's nothing to do with me but I'd feel sort of gross not saying anything.

Nancy No. Thanks. Glad you did. Everyone's sort of pretty committed to coping on their own at this point. So it's like. It's nice to like. Yeah.

David You sure you don't mind?

Miriam I don't.

David You're sure?

Miriam I'm perfectly happy to go first.

Elizabeth readies to take a swab from Miriam.

Elizabeth My daughter was asking me about your job.

David Oh really?

Elizabeth She's a maths nut.

David There's a phrase you don't hear very often. How old is she?

Elizabeth She's sixteen.

David She should come visit us at the office.

Elizabeth She would jump at the chance.

David Well I'm being serious.

Elizabeth She would bite your hand off.

David There's not much to see – Lots of computers.

Elizabeth She'll be in her element.

David She's sixteen and she likes maths?

Elizabeth She's obsessed by it. She reads these books – These great, big books full of sums and numbers.

David Shit.

Elizabeth My other two are convinced she's adopted.

Elizabeth takes a swab from the inside of Miriam's mouth.

Okay?

Miriam All good.

Elizabeth (*to David*) Ready?

David Yeah. Yeah, no. Yeah.

Elizabeth readies to take a swab from David.

I'm really impressed your daughter's . . . so into . . .

Beat.

Miriam David?

David What?

Elizabeth is ready to swab David. Beat.

Sorry.

Elizabeth It's not a problem. Take your time.

David readies himself.

David I haven't brushed my teeth.

Elizabeth It's really not a problem.

David checks his breath by cupping his hand, covering his mouth and breathing out.

David Sorry.

Elizabeth It's not a problem.

Beat.

Ready?

David readies himself.

David Mouths are such a, fucking . . . I've always thought I'm glad I'm not a hygienist –

David drops his head into his hands, upset, tearful. Beat. Pulls himself together.

Sorry.

Miriam Stop apologising.

David I'm sorry.

Elizabeth Take your time.

David I don't know what's wrong with me.

Miriam D'you want a drink?

David No thanks.

Miriam Snack?

David It's like all of a sudden my mouth is his mouth.

Beat. David retches.

I'm okay.

David retches.

Miriam Let me go and –

David No – Don't. Stay.

Miriam I should get you a –

David Will you – Could you just hold my hand for a second.

David holds out a hand, Miriam obliges. Beat.

Miriam Breathe.

Beat.

David Can I have a hug.

Miriam obliges. David's really into it, Miriam less so. They separate.

Okay. I think I'm gonna go and make myself sick –

Miriam David!

David No, in a good way, in a good way. And then I'll brush my teeth. And then, we can, let's get on and . . .

David leaves the scene. Beat.

Miriam Jesus, what a pussy.

But alas Miriam's joke falls a little flat. Beat.

Can I, d'you mind if I ask, how many . . . of these have you been involved with, Elizabeth?

Elizabeth You mean –

Miriam Missing persons.

Elizabeth Three.

Miriam What happened?

Elizabeth They were all runaways and they were all found.

Miriam Really they were all . . . ?

Elizabeth The latter two within forty-eight hours.

Miriam And the third?

Elizabeth hesitates.

You can say, it's okay.

Elizabeth She was from quite an unsavoury household. But she was found, thankfully, within a week or two of her disappearance.

Miriam Then what?

Elizabeth Her parents were charged, sentenced. And, if memory serves, she was taken in by a relative.

Miriam The other two?

Elizabeth They were already in care.

Miriam Why do you do it?

Elizabeth Helping people. The opportunity to be a part of a major investigation.

Beat.

How are you, Miriam?

Miriam How am I?

Elizabeth Yes.

Beat.

Miriam I could murder a drink? I used to be a real drinker.

Elizabeth I see.

Miriam Karl, who you spoke to? My first husband.

Elizabeth Yes, yeah.

Miriam The two of us used to get absolutely shit-faced.

Elizabeth The priest?

Miriam He's a vicar but yeah. We got sober and he found God. Shocker. I haven't had a drink since . . . I mean I used to keep track of the days. But I don't do that anymore. Rather than feeling like a badge of honour, it started to feel like a prison sentence.

Beat.

You've three kids, Elizabeth, is that right?

Elizabeth Oh yes.

Miriam With Nancy, my eldest, fuck I was terrified.

Elizabeth Oh really?

Miriam Oh my God, petrified. I wasn't necessarily someone . . . I'd never really thought of myself as being particularly maternal? My mum was a . . . I don't know. She was a complicated woman.

Elizabeth It can be tough.

Miriam With Nancy I had to be induced. Felt as if I'd done something wrong? Which I know is ridiculous. But right from the get-go she was an – (*Corrects herself.*) They. They were an amazing sleeper. Oh my God, they slept like a dream.

Elizabeth Oh really?

Miriam Six, seven hours a night, straight through.

Elizabeth Oh wow.

Miriam Miracle baby. Margaret was the opposite. She wouldn't sleep. Breastfeeding was impossible. And then with Oscar, I thought, okay, I'm ready, we can do this. But early on he developed quite a lot of allergies. At one point he lost quite a lot of weight. And he wouldn't stop crying. At night. At night would be the worst. And we tried everything, I mean, sleep training, at one point we even tried one of those night nanny people. You could really see his ribs. Because of the weight loss. And one night, he was crying, and I was all on my own, David was away. And he was crying, and he wouldn't stop. I could feel myself losing it. And I screamed. And I, I think because I must have been so tense, I farted. Loud. And he laughed. And so I, I started making farting sounds. You know – (*Demonstrates fart sound.*) And instead of crying he started laughing. And so for about the next, I mean I don't even know how long, I stayed by his cot and I made fart sounds until he fell asleep.

Beat (a long one?).

Elizabeth, where is my son?

Elizabeth considers her response (maybe this is the longer beat?).

Elizabeth We are in the process of developing a number of hypotheses.

Miriam Is he safe?

Elizabeth considers her response.

Did I do something wrong?

Elizabeth considers her response.

What if telling him about the divorce was a mistake?

Elizabeth Honesty is always the best policy.

Miriam What if he thinks I'm a monster? What if he left because he couldn't bear the thought of a lifetime with a madwoman?

Beat.

I wish there was a word.

Elizabeth A word?

Miriam A noun. To define it.

Beat.

Pool. I feel like a pool.

Elizabeth A pool?

Miriam A pool of water.

Beat. David returns to the scene with a paperback copy of The Strangest Man *by Graham Farmelo.*

David For your daughter. She might've heard of him, or maybe she won't've. But this is far and away the best biography. Couldn't get enough of him when I was her age.

David passes the book to Elizabeth.

Elizabeth Thank you, David.

Miriam All right?

David I am.

Elizabeth Ready?

Elizabeth takes a swab from the inside of David's mouth.

Thank you.

David That's it?

Elizabeth All done. I'll just be a moment.

Elizabeth leaves the scene. Beat.

David All right?

Miriam Uh-huh. You?

Beat.

What's the book about?

David This guy Paul Dirac? He was an engineering graduate who studied mathematics at Cambridge in the twenties. He was big into electrons. Apparently the only time anyone ever saw him cry was when Einstein died.

Miriam Sounds like a riot.

David He has a commemorative stone inside Westminster Abbey, next to Isaac Newton? I took Oscar to see it when Mum was in hospital.

Miriam I remember.

David It didn't exactly set his world on fire. But the bao place we went to after was top-drawer, so every cloud.

Beat.

Thanks. By the way. I keep meaning to say that.

Miriam What for?

David Everything. But. Specifically. Just then. Looking after me. I know things between us have been somewhat . . .

Miriam . . . Nightmarish?

David Uh . . .

Miriam Catastrophic?

David Well . . .

Miriam Obstinate.

David Yeah I mean we don't necessarily need to label it. I just mean. I know that I wouldn't know how to go through this on my own. Without you.

Karl *How are you, David?*

David *Me?*

Karl *Yeah.*

David *How am I?*

Karl *Yeah.*

David *I don't know.*

Karl *How are you feeling?*

David *I don't know – Spiritually you mean?*

Karl *If you want.*

David *Or how are my emotions you mean?*

Karl *Yeah.*

David *I dunno.*

Beat.

I've been watching a lot of pornography?

Karl laughs but David isn't joking.

Karl *Okay.*

David *How does the church feel about masturbation these days?*

Karl *Um.*

David *Is there an official stance?*

Karl *I think the ideal is for any sexual activity to be within the confines of a loving, lifelong relationship.*

David *Is it a sin?*

Karl *Masturbation?*

David *Pornography.*

Karl doesn't know what to say.

What about masturbating as part – Beating each other off, that sort of thing?

Karl *Within a marriage?*

David *Yeah.*

Karl *Scripture-wise, off the top of my head, I would say you're probably good to go.*

David *Oh really?*

Karl *To be honest with you, I've never really given it that much thought.*

David *Do you miss it?*

Karl *Masturbation?*

David *Any of it.*

Karl *Um, I don't – I don't have to miss it.*

David *Oh really?*

Karl *No – I don't abstain from –*

David *Oh you don't?*

Karl *No.*

David *Oh. I thought – Because you've been single for –*

Karl *I'm not a Catholic priest, David.*

Miriam enters the scene.

Miriam *There's something I need to show you.*

Miriam hands David a sheet or two of A4 paper, maybe more (printouts of email correspondence), then the same for Karl. They read for a beat.

David *This is a joke, right?*

Miriam *Finish reading it.*

Beat as he does.

David *Do you have the photos?*

Miriam hands David and Karl another sheet or two of A4 paper.

Miriam *I ignored the first few emails – But she persisted.*

David *It says here you're going to go over?*

Miriam *I am.*

David *To Ghent?*

Miriam *Yes.*

David *You're seriously gonna go over to Ghent instead of coming to the memorial? The same weekend the memorial is happening, instead of coming, you've decided you're gonna go off –*

Miriam *That's right. I'm sorry. It was a difficult decision but –*

David *No it wasn't – It wasn't even remotely difficult for you –*

Miriam *Actually that's not true –*

David *Who is she, this this this woman?*

Miriam *She used to volunteer at the library.*

David *What?*

Miriam *His favourite library, the one he used to go to, she used to volunteer. She remembers him.*

Karl *Yeah it – she says I mean, she remembers seeing you on TV.*

Miriam *She's retired now.*

David *In Ghent.*

Miriam *In Ghent. And she saw somebody, in a local –*

David *She's actually retired in actual fucking Ghent?*

Miriam *Yes.*

David *What about the police, I mean this is insane why wouldn't she –*

Miriam *She told the police and then she went on the website.*

Karl *Says here she went on the website.*

David *She told the police?*

Miriam *She told the police over there and I've spoken with the police over here.*

David *What'd they say?*

Miriam *They said it's complicated.*

David *And so this is, this is really, you're really going to go, this is for real?*

Miriam *I am, it is.*

David *Alone?*

Miriam *Yes.*

David *On your own?*

Miriam *Yes. The police will be slow, I don't want to wait.*

David *Fucking hell, Miriam, fuck would he be doing in Ghent?*

Miriam *If you wanted to come with me, David, you would be more than welcome.*

Karl *For what it's worth, I would be more than happy to come with you.*

David *She could be a lunatic, you realise that?*

Miriam *It's true, she could be.*

David *Come on, you know what I mean – Remember the woman from Reading? The bloke from Cheam? The couple from Beverley? Nutcases with nothing better to do –*

Karl *She's pretty articulate for a lunatic. Sorry, nutcase.*

David *How do you know she's not after money?*

Miriam *I don't. I don't know that. But –*

David *She could know this, this boy, this boy in the café – Couldn't she?*

Miriam *She could.*

David *They might be trying to lure you over there. In cahoots – The two of the—*

Miriam *Okay, look –*

David *I mean fuck me, Miriam – This is – This is – What even is this? It doesn't even look like him! So you'll countenance going to Ghent but not a memorial, is that really what we're saying here?*

Beat.

I wonder if you ought to speak to someone – Get some – I think – You've obviously been –

Miriam *You are – I spent – Unbelievable! – You know full well how long I spent –*

Karl *Guys –*   **David** *Please don't yell at me, M—*

Miriam *All we are talking about is a journey to Brussels – And then it is a train ride to Ghent – And then at most it is one or two nights in a hotel –*

David *But the – Stress – The strain – Look at you –*

Miriam *It is four or five days of my life – It is nothing. You should know, David, I would traverse the North Sea if –*

David *Well now you're being hysterical.*

Miriam *No; I'm being hyperbolic in order to illustrate my point, there's a difference –*

David *You're also being a pedant.*

Miriam *And you're being a ballsack.*

David *What?*

Miriam *You're being a big hairy fucking useless sack of balls, David.*

David *Wonderful.*

Karl *All right –*

Miriam *What difference does it make to you whether or not – Why are you so unwilling to support –*

Karl *Why don't we –*

David *The difference it makes, Miriam –*

Miriam *No you know what, you need to stop talking now –*

David *Miriam, come on –*	**Miriam** *No I am done with you I want you to stop moving your mouth NOW.*

Beat.

Miriam *I read about a woman – Years ago – I think it was in – Doesn't matter. Point being a young woman –*

David *Okay, I think –*

Miriam *What did I just say to you?*

Beat.

This is years ago. Decades ago. And she had sex with a pilot – At an airbase. The pilot and the young woman had sex and when the young woman's father found out, as punishment, he drove the girl, his daughter, and her pet dog, her pet fucking dog David, way out into the desert. He dragged his daughter and the dog from the car, gave his daughter a gun and ordered her to shoot the dog.

David *This is –*

Miriam *And the daughter, she cried and she begged and said she that was sorry – Said she would never do it again –*

Over and over – But her father wasn't interested – He said, take the gun and shoot the dog. But she couldn't, she wouldn't, she refused. So instead she took the gun and she blew her own brains out.

David *What the fuck, Miriam, what the in the actual fuck –*

Miriam *I'm not interested in moving on, David, and you know what else I'm not interested in, David, you're right, memorials or fucking vigils or mourning or closure or toning it down or keeping a lid on it, or time healing my wounds. I like my wounds. Time can go fuck itself and you can too you cowardly piece of fucking shit! Fuck you!*

David *All right. All right. Enough. This is insane. You're insane. She's insane. I don't know how to do this. You're impossible. She's impossible. Stop it, stop talking! STOP FUCKING TALKING!*

Karl *David. David. Miriam. I think . . .*

Nancy at the piano practising their own original composition, 'Echoes'.

Nancy
I called you up today
An echo across –

Stops. Tries again.

I called you up today
An echo on the waves
Evidence of you
Long since waylaid.

Oh to get to know you better
But maybe you wouldn't like me
Maybe we wouldn't like what we'd find
But I'll keep calling you up
A plea across the waves
'Cause even if we didn't like what we found
Either would be fine by me
Since knowing you better
Is better than knowing nothing at all

Karl Wow. That was incredible. 'S that a new one?

Nancy Work in progress.

Karl Sounded like the real deal to me.

Nancy Hi Dad.

They embrace.

What're you doing here?

Karl Well. Me and your mum we went for a drink.

Nancy I don't understand?

Miriam Soft drink.

Karl Thought I'd stop by and say hi.

Nancy Did she tell you 'bout Beverley?

Karl Amongst other things.

Nancy How is it? The hand.

Miriam Much better thank you. At this point it's the gnome I feel sorry for.

Karl How are you, Nancy?

Nancy Fantastic. You?

Karl Can't complain.

   Beat.

Nancy Why do I feel like I'm about to be noodled?

Miriam Mags told me you wanna have a séance.

Nancy What is it with this family and the like, never-ending indirect extraction of information? It's like –

Miriam She's worried about you. We both are.

Nancy I'm not some insane person you know.

Miriam Listen, we come in peace. No one is suggesting –

Nancy I went on a date with Mia and we were talking –

Miriam Mia the girl from the –

Nancy Mum she's not a girl, she's –

Miriam You know what I mean, to me she's –

Nancy Mia she works with Anil, yeah, we went on a date and she was telling me about this whole like –

Karl How was the date?

Nancy What?

Karl The date. I'm saying, how was it.

Nancy Yeah. Fine. Yeah. We ate. We drank. We –

Miriam What'd you drink?

Nancy Beer. Wine. Couple of cocktails. We went back to her place and there were meatballs so we ate meatballs.

Miriam Home-made or –

Nancy What difference does it make whether or not the –

Miriam I'm just trying to build up a picture –

Nancy Fuck me you're weird sometimes.

Miriam I'll take that as a compliment.

Nancy Yes, the meatballs were home-made. She's part Swedish.

Karl Where does she stand on Ikea?

Nancy The food or the furniture?

Karl I think there's every chance I might be addicted to those little cinnamon buns.

Nancy Yeah they're insane.

Miriam Mags said you spent the night?

Nancy Not that it's any of your business but yeah. I did.

Miriam Relax. I'm glad you had a nice time.

Nancy Well I'm glad you're glad because yeah it was pretty great actually.

Miriam Good. I'm glad to hear it.

Nancy How are things with you and David?

Miriam I wish David and Lorraine nothing but love and luck. Listen. I'm not here to try and change your mind. I went through a phase of googling psychics almost non-stop, so I understand the need. But it's not something I want your sister to be a part of –

Nancy You really used to google psychics?

Miriam I went to see one. Two if you include the one online.

Karl True story.

Nancy Jesus. What was it like?

Miriam The online one was pretty harmless.

Nancy The one in person?

Miriam Janis. At one point I got a little freaked out. She wasn't very impressed.

Nancy Why, what happened?

Miriam She did the thing with the cards? And I started to laugh, I got the giggles, she got quite angry –

Nancy Janis.

Miriam When she turned over the next card, she really let me have it.

Nancy Why, what was the next card?

Miriam I got the giggles during the High Priestess. And the one I left on was called the Hanged Man.

Nancy Left, what d'you mean?

Miriam Got up, walked out.

Nancy Why?

Beat.

(*To Karl.*) You think it's a bad idea?

Karl Psychics or meatballs?

Nancy You know what I mean.

Karl Listen, the church and spiritualism, they go way back. Personally I wouldn't touch any of that stuff with a bargepole. Steer well clear would be my advice.

Nancy Did it help? Going to see someone like Janis I mean.

Miriam It helped to finally be able to cross it off the list yeah.

David Miriam?

Miriam Yes. What? Sorry.

David Elizabeth's ready.

Miriam Right. Sorry.

Elizabeth Don't be.

Elizabeth is holding an envelope.

There are now approximately seventy or so officers working on this investigation: forty detectives and around thirty or so specialist search officers. Over two hundred hours of CCTV footage has been collected. Specialist search dogs and air support have been searching and will continue to search houses and open ground within a five-hundred-metre radius of the school. Which brings me to this. (*Meaning envelope.*) It was found in the toilet of a petrol station three-quarters of a mile from the school.

Miriam The Esso or the other one?

Elizabeth The Esso, that's right. Inside this envelope there are six photographs, exterior and interior of the wallet. All I need you to do is to take a look at the photographs and confirm for me that you recognise this item as belonging to Oscar.

Beat.

If I might make a suggestion?

David Please.

Elizabeth I would suggest starting with you, Miriam, followed by David. Followed by Nancy, followed by Margaret.

Miriam Fine by me.

Elizabeth David?

David Sure.

Miriam Okay.

Elizabeth hands the envelope to Miriam and she takes out the photographs (the envelope is not sealed).

Miriam looks at the first photograph and shows it to David. Miriam and David look through the remaining photographs together. They then pass the photographs on to Nancy and Margaret. This takes as long as it takes.

It's empty.

Elizabeth Yes.

David You mean – Sorry, the wallet was empty when you found it you mean?

Elizabeth Correct.

Miriam What happened to the contents?

Elizabeth We don't know.

Miriam Why would it be empty?

Elizabeth We don't know, I'm sorry.

David Did somebody take it d'you think?

Elizabeth We don't know, I'm sorry.

Miriam Take it, what do you mean? Why would somebody –

David Steal it. Did somebody steal his wallet and take all the –

Miriam Why would somebody steal a wallet from a child?

David Why do people do anything?

Miriam So you found the wallet, but when you found the wallet everything inside it was gone?

Elizabeth Correct.

Miriam Everything inside it was gone, and you've no idea where any of it might be?

Elizabeth Correct.

Miriam Or why or how it was even there in the first place?

Elizabeth Correct.

David Which is what I'm saying, it's either empty because somebody stole it, or it's empty because, I dunno, he took everything he needed –

Miriam But why would he be at a petrol station? What would he be doing at a petrol station?

Margaret Maybe he wanted an ice cream?

David Well you said it was in a toilet, maybe he was just –

Miriam But don't they, sorry, don't the people who, don't they have any kind of CCTV?

Elizabeth Unfortunately, the toilets, which are external, aren't covered by CCTV.

Miriam So he never went inside the actual, the thing, the shop?

David Well that's – You're assuming he was even there in the first place?

Elizabeth At the moment there's ultimately no way of knowing for certain one way or the other. I'm sorry.

Beat.

Margaret It's definitely his. By the way.

Nancy Yeah.

Margaret It was a Christmas present from us, so.

Beat: Margaret grows upset. David and Nancy comfort her, Miriam does not. Perhaps photographs are returned to envelope.

Miriam So what happens now, I mean what's next?

Elizabeth Well, with your permission, we'd like to release the CCTV image of Oscar outside the school. What's more . . . We would like to organise a press conference.

Miriam Really?

David With us?

Elizabeth Yes. But only if you were comfortable – If you were comfortable making a, yes, a short statement, we feel it would be –

Miriam Absolutely. I mean I would be, but –

David All of us? You mean all of us, or you mean –

Elizabeth It doesn't have to be. Again, whatever you feel comfortable doing, then that's what we'll do.

Margaret I saw this thing on YouTube and the family were all wearing T-shirts?

Elizabeth That's right. Sometimes, though not always –

Nancy Will we have to wear T-shirts?

David I think I'd rather not – If that's all right with everyone?

Margaret There was a line of people wearing T-shirts with a photo and the word 'missing' running across their chests.

David That does sound weird.

Elizabeth We can say no to T-shirts.

Nancy I don't wanna do it, I'm sorry.

Miriam That's fine.   **David** The T-shirt or the –

Nancy I really don't wanna have to go on TV, I think it's disgusting I'm sorry.

Miriam You don't have to.

Nancy I'm sorry.

Miriam You don't need to apologise.

Elizabeth We don't need to reach a decision right now.

Miriam (*meaning she and David*) No but I think we should, I think we should do it. I think at the very least it should be the two of us.

David Agreed.

Miriam Don't you think? I think we should be there. I think we should do it.

David I'm agreeing with you.

Miriam Good, I'm glad that you're agreeing with me.

Beat.

David The only thing I'm wondering – (*To Miriam.*) Don't look at me like that. All I'm wondering, is how we're gonna – If we address it at all, that is, how we –

Miriam I don't understand, address what?

Margaret Mum just let him finish.

David What will we do about the divorce?

Miriam What?

David If I saw a couple on TV – For example – If I saw a couple on TV, making a, whatever you want to call it, and I knew they were separating –

Miriam David, it is nobody's –

David No but I'm saying I wonder if I would take the whole thing a little less seriously.

Miriam Why? We don't have to be together in order to love our son.

David But isn't – Aren't we – Isn't the idea that we want people to sit up –

Miriam We don't have to be perfect parents in order to love our son, David –

David I'm talking about me personally. My response. What my own personal response might be, if I saw two people, or however many, appealing for my – All I'm trying to question is whether I might think to myself, well, if things at home aren't great, maybe the problem isn't –

Miriam What in the holy fuck are you talking about.

Nancy Mum.   **Margaret** Mum.

Miriam *We're* responsible, is that –

David No, that is –

Miriam It's *our* fault, is that –

David No – You are twisting – That is not –

Miriam The state of our marriage is no one's business but our –

David I know that! I mean I know that for Christ's sake! But shock horror Miriam not everyone might feel that way. And get ready to have your world view shattered because sometimes, sometimes people make snap-fucking-judgements about people they barely know –

Miriam I don't care. I don't care what happens to me and I don't care what people think of me –

David Well you ought to, you ought to care what people think of you, Miriam, because if all people think when they see us is we had it coming, then they're not gonna help. They're not gonna give two shits.

Miriam If people think getting divorced makes you an incapable parent then they can go and fuck themselves.

David Brilliant. I think we're ready, let's get the cameras in here now.

Margaret Please please stop talking like this, please, it just –

Nancy Agreed.

Miriam All right. All right. You're right. I'm sorry. I'm sorry.

Elizabeth Look. It's entirely possible. It's important . . . There'll be no going back, that's for sure.

David I'm going to do it. I've said that. I just want to make sure that whatever we do is as effective as it possibly can be. That's all. That's all I'm trying to do. I'm prepared to do whatever it takes. I mean it. My commitment here is un-fucking-wavering.

Miriam *Would anybody like anything else to drink? Wine? Beer? Juice?*

Everyone shakes their heads politely and says 'No', 'No thank you', et cetera. Awkward beat. David receives a text message, checks his smartphone:

David *Three minutes away. Says the traffic's easing up.*

Miriam *Lucky us.*

Awkward beat.

David *So you two, where are we up to with names?*

Benjamin *Uh . . .*

Margaret *It's a process.*

Benjamin *I'd say the decision-making process is like definitely on-going.*

David *Any favourites Benjamin?*

Margaret *Dad.*

David *What. It's exciting. I'm excited.*

David receives a text message:

One and a half.

Beat.

I remember when we were tryina choose a name for you it was like World War fucking Three.

Beat.

Benjamin *Maybe it's okay to say about. 'Cause we've ruled it out. But at one point I was quite into the idea of Maya. But Mags thinks –*

Margaret *I just think it's maybe weird to have the same first initial as your kid. (To Miriam.) No offence.*

Miriam *Margaret was my grandmother's name.*

Margaret *It's a great name. I'm just saying.*

Beat.

David *Guess that rules out Bamm-Bamm.*

Benjamin *Oh wow are you a* Flintstones *fan David?*

David *Well. I mean. Not anymore. But. Back in the day.*

Benjamin *I used to love* The Flintstones.

Beat.

Did you ever see – There was this spin-off? Pebbles and Bamm-Bamm are like teenagers and they're dating. They're in secondary school and they've hooked up. It was pretty wild.

Lorraine joins the scene.

Lorraine *Hi! Hi! Hi everyone, I am so, so sorry I'm so late.*

Everyone is polite, friendly and welcoming, Miriam cool. Lorraine, sincerely affectionate, hugs, kisses everyone:

(To Margaret.) So lovely to see you, congratulations! Again! (To Benjamin.) Benjamin, lovely to see you again.

(*To David.*) *Fancy seeing you here.* (*To Miriam.*) *Miriam.* (*Hands Miriam bottle.*) *Non-alcoholic sparkling kombucha. Little something to get the party started.*

Miriam *What can we get you to drink, Lorraine? Wine? Beer? Juice?*

Lorraine *Wine. Yes please.*

Miriam *Red or white?*

Lorraine *Whatever's easiest.*

Miriam *Red or white?*

Lorraine *Red please.*

  Beat.

Well. Cheers. Here's to you two.

  Awkward toast.

Exciting.

  Beat.

So. How have we been getting on with names?

  Beat. David perhaps gives Lorraine a discreet signal that they've already covered that topic.

And remind me, boy or girl? Or top secret?

Miriam *Actually – Sorry, Lorraine, I think you might have something – In your . . .*

  She's referring to (*bit of food stuck in*) *Lorraine's teeth. Lorraine tries to address this.*

. . . Right at the front.

  Beat.

Benjamin *I think we're probably up for a surprise.*

Margaret *Totally.*

Lorraine *Lucky dip. I like your style.*

Miriam (*to Lorraine*) *Actually – Sorry – I can still see it.*

David *Fuck is wrong with you?*

Miriam *I'm just saying, we have toothpicks.*

Beat.

Lorraine *And have you thought any more about life insurance?*

Miriam *Jesus, keep it light Lorraine. That was a joke, that was a joke. I come in peace.*

Margaret *Yeah. I mean. Kind of.*

Benjamin *It's definitely something we wanna get to.*

Lorraine *Critical illness is the other one that's really worth thinking about.*

Beat.

The great thing about critical illness is that it can be undertaken as a standalone policy or jointly combined with a new or pre-existing life insurance policy.

Beat.

Well look I'm here. And you know I'd love to help.

Margaret *Yeah. No. Cool. Thanks.*

Benjamin *Definitely.*

Beat.

Lorraine *I was talking to a –*

Miriam *I was sorry to hear about your father, Lorraine.*

Lorraine *Oh. Thank you.*

Miriam *Cancer. What a cunt.*

Beat.

David said everything went well with the funeral though.

Lorraine It did. Thank you.

Beat.

Miriam *I've always thought I'd like to just be fired off into space.*

Beat.

David *So Benjamin, what are you um working on at the moment?*

Margaret *Dad –*

Benjamin *Uh, still the, the same, I'm still working for the –*

David *Yeah no, I know – I wasn't – Specifically, what is that you're specifically –*

Benjamin *Oh, right, sorry, yeah. I'm, uh, it's a, it's a research project, revolving, um, involving, looking at the world's declining puffin population?*

Lorraine *Puffins?*

Benjamin *Yeah.*

Lorraine *The bird?*

Benjamin *Yeah.*

Lorraine *Puffins as in the birds –*

Benjamin *They're a seabird but yeah.*

Lorraine *Oh my God I love puffins.*

Benjamin *Oh really oh wow that's so great.*

Lorraine *Yeah my dad was a real bird-watcher when I was a little girl, so. How wonderful. I mean not that they're in decline! But that that's how you get to spend your time.*

Benjamin *There's been a lot of concern recently about the – And I mean not just here. Internationally, too.*

Lorraine *I'll bet.*

Benjamin *Yeah they're not quite endangered – Yet – In the UK – but they're getting pretty close.*

Lorraine *Awful.*

Benjamin *We don't have as much data as like, as we'd like, but estimates suggest the global puffin population has dropped by like over half, in the last like fifty years.*

Lorraine *Awful.*

Miriam *Awful.*

Benjamin *Puffins, they have like –*

Margaret *Benny.*

Benjamin *What? Oh sorry, am I – I didn't mean to –*

Lorraine *Oh my goodness don't be silly. Honestly it's fascinating. I'm a big big animal lover my love so you're preaching to the choir.*

Benjamin *They have two like, pretty distinct phases of existence?*

Lorraine *Oh right.*

Benjamin *So as a result they're like – Yeah they're like a sort of weirdly good indicator of how climate change is really messing with marine biodiversity.*

Lorraine *I'll bet.*

Benjamin *They spend four months-ish on land, breeding.*

Lorraine *Lucky puffins.*

Benjamin *Then they spend yeah, the rest of the year out at sea. And it's like, in order to feed their pufflings – Because – Sorry – Jumping around –*

Lorraine *Now wait a minute. Did you just say pufflings? Did he just say pufflings?*

Margaret *He did.*

Benjamin *Yeah puffin chicks they're known as pufflings.*

Lorraine *Oh my goodness that's adorable.*

Margaret *I've seen pictures. They're pretty cute.*

Lorraine *Pufflings, I love that.*

Benjamin *Yeah they, so the females they raise only, they only raise one chick a year?*

Lorraine *All right for some.*

Benjamin *One egg. So the viability of the colony is like, pretty precarious. Depends on a lot of factors working together in synchronicity in order for the pufflings to, like, survive, if you see what I'm saying.*

Lorraine *Completely.*

Benjamin *Over-fishing, extreme weather.*

Lorraine *Don't get me started, Benjamin, honestly.*

Benjamin *There's a particular kind of cold-water zooplankton which has been in decline since the 1980s 'cause of the rise in sea temperatures?*

Lorraine *Awful.*

Benjamin *And this particular kind of cold-water zooplankton, it used to get eaten by this like particular type of sand eel?*

Lorraine *Oh right.*

Benjamin *But as this particular plankton has gone into decline, it's had a knock-on effect on the sand eel population . . .*

Margaret *Because puffins like eating sand eels.*

Benjamin *It's a puffling staple for sure.*

Lorraine *Well I'll bet.*

Benjamin *So if there aren't enough sand eels, or the sand eels have moved too far away from, like, the burrows and breeding grounds, basically what we're seeing is pufflings starving to death.*

Miriam OH MY GOD JESUS FUCKING CHRIST ENOUGH. *Enough. I mean for fuck's sake, enough. I mean fuck ME somebody change the fucking subject –*

Margaret *Oh my God please don't do this. Not now.*	**David** *All right – All right – It's all right – Everybody's all right . . .*

Miriam *I swear to God I'm gonna open a fucking vein if I have to listen to any more –*

David *Miriam, Miriam –*	**Margaret** *Mum what the fuck!*

Miriam *I'm sorry but it's just on and on and on and on and on and on and on – I mean who GIVES A SHIT –*

David *Miriam, come on. Be reasonable –*	**Margaret** *Mum. Please.*

Lorraine *No d'you know what? It's okay. It's all right. It is, it's okay to let off a little steam. It is. It's important. After everything you've been through. Miriam. Endured. All of you. It's a lot. The pain. Suffering. Let alone the harassment. Abuse. The press. Everything you must be having to process on a daily basis. The courage that must take. I mean honestly. All of you. Truly.*

Miriam *Finally. Thank you. Lorraine. Because sometimes it can feel like. This lot they don't really get me, you know? And it's like sometimes all I want is a hug.*

    Beat.

Word on the street Lorraine is you give out a pretty great hug.

David *Listen to me –*

Lorraine *It's okay, it's all right. Miriam. Of course. I'd be more than happy to give you a hug right now. If that's something you feel you need –*

Miriam *Yes please.*

David *You don't need to do anything you're not a hundred per cent comfortable doing –*

Lorraine *It's just a hug David.*

Miriam *Yeah David it's just a hug. You see what I'm saying, Lorraine, this is what I'm up against when it comes to getting a hug these days.*

Beat.

Lorraine *Ready whenever you are.*

Miriam hugs Lorraine, Lorraine embraces Miriam. This takes as long as it takes. Everyone not participating in the hug on edge.

David *All right that's enough now . . .*

The hug continues. Everyone not participating in the hug on edge.

All right, come on. Come on that's enough.

Miriam tightens her grip on Lorraine.

Miriam if you don't let go –

Lorraine *It's okay, it's all right. Miriam. This is starting to hurt a little –*

Miriam tightens her grip on Lorraine –

All right that's enough now Miriam please stop –

Margaret *Stop. Mum. Enough.*

David *Miriam I swear to God if you don't let go –*

Nancy Mum.

Miriam tightens her grip –

Lorraine *Ow, ow – Okay this is really starting to hurt now – David please help –*

Nancy Mum.

David sets about trying to prise Miriam off Lorraine. Margaret too tries to help.

David *Let fucking go! Let fucking go of her!*	**Margaret** *Mum! Please! I don't understand what you're doing why won't you stop?!*

Finally, David and Margaret manage to extract Lorraine from Miriam's grip.

David *Fuck is wrong with you?!*

Miriam *Just letting off a little steam a little steam what's wrong with a little steam.* (*A toast.*) *To a little steam –*

Nancy Mum!

Miriam What? Yes. Sorry. I was miles away.

David *You're a psycho you're an actual bona fide psycho d'you know that!*

Nancy Ready?

David *We're leaving, let's go. It's not safe, you're not safe.*

Miriam Yes. What? Sorry.

Mia I just wanted to check whether there are any more questions or if you're both okay to start?

Miriam Me? Yes.

Mia Okay, great. Let's sit.

They do so, at a table.

And let's, whenever you're ready, I'm going to ask you to place your hands on the table.

They do so.

Great, thanks. Everybody still okay?

Nancy nods.

Great. Miriam, okay, comfortable?

Miriam nods.

Great. So okay so yeah, so what I'd like us to do next is just to concentrate.

Beat.

For a moment.

Beat.

Still. Silent.

Beat.

I'd like us just to have his name in our heads. Maybe even saying it a couple of times.

Nancy Out loud?

Mia No, sorry, just. Inside.

Beat.

And still remembering – I mean trying still to not put too much pressure on the table.

Beat.

Okay, ready?

Nodding.

I'd like to invite anyone that is in the room with us to make themselves known.

Beat.

In particular – We would be particularly interested to hear from Oscar. Oscar Wright.

Beat.

We would be particularly interested to hear from Oscar Wright.

Beat.

If you're in the room with us Oscar, we would love to hear from you.

Beat.

You can use our energy to move the table.

Beat.

Oscar, if you are in the room with us, please feel free to use our energy to move the table.

Beat.

Once again, we would be particularly interested to hear from you. Oscar Wright. If you are in the room with us, please feel free to move our – Sorry, to *use* our energy. To yeah, to move the table.

Beat.

Nancy Should we stop?

Mia Honestly up to you.

Nancy I think maybe I'd like to try keeping going.

Mia Okay, great. Miriam?

Beat.

Nancy Mum.

Miriam What? Yes. Sorry.

Beat.

Mia So okay so we'd like to check. To double check. Oscar Wright. If you are in the room with us, we'd love to hear from you.

Beat.

Because we'd like to ask you a couple of questions.

Beat.

I'm here with Nancy and your mother, Oscar, and they have some things they would like to ask.

Beat.

Nancy Oscar. Hi. Uhm it's Nancy.

Beat.

How are you?

Beat.

Oscar, was that you I saw in my bedroom?

Beat.

Mia Ask again.

Nancy Oscar, was that you that I saw in my bedroom?

Beat.

Beside the piano.

Beat.

So that wasn't you I saw in my bedroom beside the piano?

Beat.

(*More difficult than anticipated.*) Oscar, did something happen to you?

Beat.

Oscar, did something happen to you?

Beat.

Did something happen to you, Oscar?

Beat.

Did somebody hurt you?

Beat.

Oscar, did somebody hurt you?

Beat.

Did somebody do something to you, Oscar?

Beat.

If somebody hurt you, or they did something to you, you can say.

Beat.

(*Becoming more difficult.*) Oscar, we love you, we love you so much, and if something happened to you, please, Oscar, we just, all we want is to know. To know. To know, Oscar, that's all we want. If somebody did something to you, Oscar, or if something hap—

Miriam All right, all right, enough, enough.

Miriam has stood up and moved away from the table, deeply upset.

Nancy All right –

Miriam Stop, just stop, just –

Nancy Okay. Okay. All right.

Miriam I'm sorry.

Mia We've stopped.

Miriam It's too. I'm too. Because why would you say that?

Nancy I dunno –

Miriam Did somebody hurt you, did something happen, why would you –

Nancy Because – I dunno! Because I guess maybe it's like – I dunno! It's like –

Miriam And so okay and so you mean. You mean. You mean. You m-m-mean – You think that, that, that, that somebody would actually want, wanted to, would have want wanted to –

Nancy I dunno. I dunno. Look. I'm sorry –

Miriam vomits.

Nancy Oh my God.   Mia Jesus.

Miriam Fine, 's fine honestly.

Nancy You don't need to – Stop – It's okay not to be –

Mia Is there anything we can –

Miriam vomits.

Mia Whoa.   Nancy Jesus, fuck.

Miriam It's okay. It's fine. I'm fine.

Nancy Mum –

Miriam I would have come to pick you up.

Nancy What?

Miriam How much was the taxi?

Nancy Wait. Wha—

Miriam Let me give you some money.

Nancy I don't under—

Miriam Have you noticed anything missing from the house?

Nancy What?   Mia Me? No –

Miriam Are you sure we can't get you something else to drink?

Nancy Mum –

Miriam It's just one of these videos that gets passed around. Teenagers these days they're all ten-a-penny. He had an ingrowing toenail. You could really see his ribs. Because of the weight loss. You couldn't just order a burger – You had to order a waffle burger, And he was crying, and he wouldn't stop and I could feel myself losing it and it was either that or throw myself off the Humber Bridge and at this point it's the gnome I feel sorry for, and then when the person when they stop tickling, it lowers its arms and rather than feeling like a badge of honour it started to feel like albumen, because why would he be at a prison sentence think really all I'm saying is that there had been some kind of isolated incident involving an account with Fuck the trolls we saw each other and everything seemed fine and he said twelve thirty-seven I guess is what we're s'posed to infer because rather than feeling like breastfeeding was impossible I used to keep track of the days but I don't do that anymore. Because we've been doing that, all of us, it was ordinary, it was all ordinary, the whole morning was ordinary and rather than feeling like a badge of honour it started to feel like when you pull out all the stops you apparently you get this blast this pool this wall of fucking –

Karl How are you, Miriam?

Miriam Me?

Karl Yeah.

Miriam How am I?

Karl How are you feeling yeah.

Miriam I dunno. I've been watching a lot of extreme makeover shows.

Karl Okay.

Miriam Hey, how was your date?

Karl How d'you know about that?

Miriam You told me.

Karl I have no memory of that.

Miriam Where did you go?

Karl Mexican place.

Miriam Any good?

Karl It was okay. One of these places where they bring the food when it's ready?

Miriam That sort of thing pisses me off no end.

Karl I don't mind it.

Miriam What was her name, your date?

Karl Ada.

Miriam And?

Karl She was a bit of a desperate mess to be honest.

Miriam Ouch.

Karl Her husband died about five years ago.

Miriam You didn't feel like taking of advantage of her?

Karl She said to me she'd always wanted to fuck a vicar.

Miriam She did not?

Karl Cross my heart.

Miriam Were you wearing the full get up?

Karl No. It says I'm a vicar on my profile.

Miriam How does the church feel about one-night stands?

Karl Well, I guess they're not exactly ideal.

Miriam We could have sex.

Karl We could, that's true.

Miriam Might be nice.

Karl Might be.

Beat.

Miriam I used to really love the insides of your thighs. Somewhere between a marshmallow and a tyre.

Karl I used to be really into the lunette of your neck. Particularly first thing in the morning.

Miriam I remember.

Karl I used to love the mornings.

Miriam What did you think of the press conference?

Karl I thought everything you had to say was extremely potent.

Miriam The internet thinks I sounded like a twat.

Karl Well I think the internet sounds like a twat.

Miriam MervynBParkRanger69 was kind enough to get in touch to let me know my face looks like a stitched-up arsehole.

Beat.

On the plus side. Elizabeth says the incident room, she says they've received over two hundred and fifty calls.

Karl Wow.

Miriam She says they're going to follow up on every single one.

Karl That's fantastic.

Miriam I keep thinking about his body.

Karl I bet.

Miriam Because his body used to be my body.

Beat.

Karl do you really still believe in God?

Karl Uh-huh, yeah, most of the time, most of the time I still really believe in God, yeah.

Miriam Why only most of the time?

Karl Well. I'm tryina make sense of the world around me. Sometimes I do, sometimes I don't.

Miriam What does it feel like? When you do.

Karl A light. A presence.

Miriam What about when you don't?

Karl Well. Faith is practice. So. I mean it's a verb. So, I pray.

Miriam What for?

Karl All sorts of things. Guidance. Support.

Miriam What about Oscar?

Karl You mean have I –

Miriam Recently.

Karl Have I prayed for Oscar recently you mean?

Miriam Yes.

Karl Every day.

Miriam And how are you feeling about the results?

Karl There's no need to take the piss –

Miriam I wasn't. I wasn't. I mean it. I wanna know.

Beat.

Karl Well. I dunno.

Beat.

I think . . .

Beat.

I s'pose I'm not so much looking for results as I am looking for . . . Looking for that presence, that charge. A way of dealing with the incompleteness of the world around me.

Miriam Because none of it makes sense?

Karl None of it makes sense and it's about learning to live with that.

Miriam And what about heaven, where do you stand on heaven?

Karl Generally speaking I feel pretty good about it.

Miriam Karl if I asked you to say a prayer with me is that something d'you think, is that something you might be up for?

Karl Definitely.

Miriam It wouldn't be weird?

Karl Why would it be weird?

Miriam Because we were just talking about marshmallows and fucking.

Karl All good.

Miriam How does it . . . What's the best . . .

Karl Well. You wanna kneel or you wanna stand . . .

Miriam You tell me.

Karl I'm fond of a kneel.

Miriam nods, they kneel.

Miriam Would you be able to hold my hands?

Karl holds Miriam's hands in his as they ready to pray.

And it's just. I mean it's okay to just say whatever I want?

Karl More than okay it's essential.

Miriam lowers her head, closes her eyes and prays. Karl does the same. This takes as long as it takes. Karl finishes before Miriam. When she is finished Miriam raises her head and opens her eyes.

Amen.

Miriam Amen.

Margaret *There was something we wanted to talk to you about before dinner.*

Miriam *Okay.*

Margaret *Please don't bristle at me.*

Miriam *I'm not.*

Margaret *You are definitely bristling.*

Miriam *Fine. Then I'll try not to.*

Margaret *Try harder. 'Cause there's every chance I'm not gonna be able to keep my shit together if you keep bristling like that.*

Beat.

We don't think you should go to Ghent.

Nancy *We want you to come to the memorial instead.*

Miriam *You don't think I should go, or you don't want me to go?*

Margaret *I don't know what the difference is? They're the same, aren't they, aren't they the same?*

Nancy *We want you to be with us. Instead.*

Miriam *(to David) Is this you? This is your fucking doing isn't it?*

David *Listen –*

Nancy *This has nothing to do with – Mum this is us. Mags called me, I called Dad – (Meaning Karl.)*

Margaret *This has nothing to do with Dad.*

Miriam *Well for the record I don't appreciate being ganged up on. By anybody.*

Karl *Nobody is here to –*

Nancy *All we want is a conversation.*

Beat.

Miriam *All right then fine – Tell me then why you don't think I should –*

Margaret *Because we're worried about you.*

Nancy *All of us.*

Miriam *Explain 'all'.*

Karl *Everyone here.*

Margaret *Isn't it obvious?*

Miriam *You're 'worried' about me.*

David *We're worried about you because we love you, Miriam.*

Miriam *Is that right.*

Margaret *Yes!*

Nancy *It is actually. All of us.*

Beat.

Miriam *Why.*

Nancy *Why do we all love you –*

David *You mean why do we all love you or why do we –*

Miriam *I mean what exactly is it that you're all so fucking worried about.*

Margaret *I'd like to point out that I still feel like I'm on the receiving end of like, quite a lot of bristling.*

Miriam *I'm doing what any parent in my position would do.*

Margaret *Maybe. I dunno. I guess I wouldn't know about that.*

Miriam *Correct. You wouldn't.*

Margaret *Oh okay. Wow. Okay. Fine. How about this, then, how about maybe the reason I don't want you to go is because, as always – And normally, fine, you can do whatever – Scream and shout and throw shit – Call me a cunt –*

Miriam *Hey, hey, I have never –*

Margaret *I mean figuratively – I'm saying figuratively speaking you've called me a cunt like a hundred times –*

Miriam *Respectfully I disagree –*

Margaret *I'm saying it doesn't matter! Because I can take it. Because I'm a fucking hero and one day I might even be able to forgive you. But, the thing is, now I've got an actual human being growing inside me, I need to know that you won't go mental in front of my child –*

Miriam *I would never –*

Margaret *Or that you're not gonna like resent it, or me, or some weird fucked up combination of the –*

Miriam *Mags, I would never –*

Margaret *But how do I know that? Mum. How can I know that? I don't want my kid to inherit all the shit.*

Miriam *I don't know what you want me to say.*

Margaret *Then maybe you ought to just listen. Because the other thing, is like, it's like. Let's say you get there. You're in fucking Ghent. And it's snowing. And it's shit. And let's say it isn't him. Then what? When it isn't him, what happens then?*

Miriam *I don't understand?*

Margaret *Please don't make me spell it out.*

Miriam *Don't make me ask you to.*

Margaret *I'm worried about what you might do to yourself when you're all alone.*

Miriam absorbs this.

David *Also. Speaking for myself –*

Miriam *Who the fuck else would you be speaking for?*

Margaret *Mum!*   **Nancy** *Jesus.*

Miriam *All right all right all right.*

David *I'm talking about me personally. My own personal preference here. I don't want a memorial or a vigil or whatever the fuck you wanna call it because I want to move on. I don't. Honest to God – But nor do I particularly wanna keep living like this. I wanna celebrate or remember or whatever the word is, all the years we did have. And crucially I wanna get under the skin of all the years we're never gonna have back. And yes I would like to do that in public, out loud. Together. And maybe fuck it I dunno, maybe he shows up. Or maybe somebody films it, you know, they're on their phone and they're filming it and it ends up, you know – And he sees it. And fuck it maybe he finally decides to pick up the phone and get in –*

Miriam *Then fine, then how about this, come with me to Ghent, rearrange the memorial –*

Nancy *Mum –*

Margaret *That isn't Dad's point and you know it.*

Miriam *No I'm serious I mean it. I would love that. All of you, come with me, and then as soon as we're back –*

Karl *I think the point maybe David's tryina make –*

Margaret *Ugh that isn't Dad's point and you know it!*

David *She's impossible – You're impossible.*

Karl *Everybody here all we want is the opportunity to be able to take care of you, Miriam. Because we love you.*

Margaret *Do you have any idea how selfish you're being right now?*

Nancy *Easy –*

Margaret *'Cause at this point . . . it's like . . .*

Flicker of upset from Margaret. Benjamin might comfort her.

Benjamin *You all right?*

Margaret *Fine.*

Benjamin *'Cause we can stop?*

Margaret *I'm fine. I s'pose I sort of feel like there are basically only two options. Either he left voluntarily, or he didn't. (Getting difficult.) And I love him. Now I love him, I mean I fucking love him . . . But if he left 'cause he wanted to, then there's a bit of me that's like: fuck you.*

Nancy *Mags –*

Margaret *No I'm gonna finish thanks.*

Beat.

I don't think we could miss him any more than we already do because that would be physically impossible. Everyone has done everything. They have. No, they have, listen to me,

Mum, they have. Everyone has done everything. You, have done, absolutely, fucking, everything. And in the meantime it's like, I just want my fucking mum back.

Beat.

I guess maybe it's just like I wish that we could be enough for you.

Miriam *It isn't just him.*
I wouldn't give up on any   **Margaret** (*on 'I'*) *I mean it's*
of you.   *like I don't even understand*
     what the fuck it is you're even
     looking for anymore?!

Miriam *Would you like me to try and explain it to you?*

Margaret *I mean, yeah, I mean sure, I mean be my fucking guest.*

Miriam *I don't have to.*

Margaret *No, you're right, you know what, please. Do. Enlighten me.*

Miriam *Well.*

Miriam takes her time, it becomes difficult for her perhaps.

Okay. I suppose I've been thinking an awful lot about his shoulders. Whether or not they might be any broader. His hair. How he might be brushing his hair. The hair on his face. Knees. Ribs. Teeth. Is he flossing properly. The skin around his thumbs, whether or not he's still biting it. Ingrown toenail. Piercings. You know? Does he have any. Tattoos. Height. Shoe size. Is he still into skating. Books, reading . . . Did he ever get to the end of Moby-Dick *or did he just give up and decide to pretend like the rest of us? Music . . . Is he still listening to the Arctic Monkeys on loop or has his taste finally evolved? Weight. Diet. Fruit. Nuts for fuck's sake. Or is he still basically carnivorous to within an inch of his life? Is he with anyone . . . who does he spend his time with . . . is he lonely without us . . . You know? But the main thing I'm looking for. I suppose. Is the chance to let him know that I'm sorry. And that whatever it is that he needs. Whatever it is that he wants. I'm ready.*

    Beat.

I love my son. My son is alive.

    Beat.

Let's eat. We should eat.

    Everyone takes a seat. Everyone serves up the meal, and everyone eats. This takes as long as it takes.